2nd October '96

5.65

Clive Barlow

SEMINAR STUDIES IN HISTORY
General Editor: Roger Lockyer

The Glorious Revolution

John Miller

Roya Devani

LONGMAN
London and New York

LONGMAN GROUP LIMITED,
Longman House, Burnt Mill, Harlow, Essex CM20 2JE, England
and Associated Companies throughout the World.

Published in the United States of America
by Longman Inc., New York

© Longman Group Limited 1983

First published 1983
Ninth impression 1995

ISBN 0 582 35366 1

Set in 10/11pt. Baskerville, Linotron 202
Produced through Longman Malaysia, CL

For my parents

British Library Cataloguing in Publication Data

Miller, John
 The Glorious Revolution.—(Seminar studies in history)
 1. William, III *King of England*
 2. Great Britain—History—Revolution of 1688
 I. Title   II. Series
 942.06'7   DA452

Library of Congress Cataloging in Publication Data

Miller, John (John Leslie)
 The glorious revolution.

 (Seminar studies, in history)
 Bibliography: p.
 Includes index.
 Summary: Discusses the causes and effects of the revolution which assured
the failure of Catholic absolutism and assured the continuation of parliamentary
government and the rule of law in England.
  1. Great Britain − − History − − Revolution of 1688.
 [1. Great Britain − − History − − Revolution of 1688]
 I. Title. II. Series.
 DA452.M55 1983 941.06'7 82–20869

Contents

Acknowledgements

We are grateful to Cambridge University Press for permission to reproduce extracts from *Eighteenth Century Constitution* by E.N. Williams.

Cover: An engraving from 'The Protestants Joy; or An Excellent New Song on the Glorious Coronation of King William and Queen Mary' from the Bagford Ballads (1689), published in 1878 by the Ballad Society. By permission of the Mansell Collection.

Seminar Studies in History
Founding Editor: Patrick Richardson

Introduction

The Seminar Studies series was conceived by Patrick Richardson, whose experience of teaching history persuaded him of the need for something more substantial than a textbook chapter but less formidable than the specialised full-length academic work. He was also convinced that such studies, although limited in length, should provide an up-to-date and authoritative introduction to the topic under discussion as well as a selection of relevant documents and a comprehensive bibliography.

Patrick Richardson died in 1979, but by that time the Seminar Studies series was firmly established, and it continues to fulfil the role he intended for it. This book, like others in the series, is therefore a living tribute to a gifted and original teacher.

Note on the System of References:
A bold number in round brackets (**5**) in the text refers the reader to the corresponding entry in the Bibliography section at the end of the book. A bold number in square brackets, preceded by 'doc.' [**doc. 6**] refers the reader to the corresponding item in the section of Documents, which follows the main text.

ROGER LOCKYER
General Editor

Preface

To most Englishmen of the eighteenth and nineteenth centuries the Revolution of 1688—9 was indeed 'glorious'. It ensured the failure of James II's attempt to establish a Catholic absolutism and made possible the continuation and extension of the great English traditions of parliamentary government and the rule of law. This view received its most magisterial statement from Lord Macaulay, who saw in the Revolution the seeds of every good and liberal law enacted in the next century and a half (**85**). The 'Whig' or liberal values of Macaulay have continued to influence historians. 'The Revolution', wrote Trevelyan, 'gave to England an ordered and legal freedom and through that it gave her power' (**115**). To David Ogg, who compared absolutism to fascism, the Revolution played a vital role in the formation of Anglo-Saxon civilisation 'maintained by communities which are as ready to defend their liberties as they are unwilling to enforce them on others' (**93**). The legacy of the Revolution was, indeed, not confined to England. One has only to read the United States constitution to see strong signs of the influence of the Revolution and of its greatest apologist, John Locke.

The last century has seen some challenges to this traditional view of the Revolution. Marxist historians have not so much challenged it as ignored the Revolution altogether. Seeing economic and social developments as the motive forces of historical change, they have applied to the events of 1640—60 the title which Acton and Trevelyan gave to 1688—9, 'the English Revolution'. Only the civil wars and their aftermath, they argued, constituted an upheaval comparable to the French and Russian revolutions, while the emergence of the Levellers, Diggers and radical sects suggested an element of class conflict, of which there was little sign in 1688. It was far from easy to fit the events of 1640—60 into the Marxist model of a 'bourgeois revolution': indeed Engels, with more historical sense than terminological precision, cast the gentry in the historical role of the 'bourgeoisie'. Nevertheless many historians, convinced that such great events must have had their source in profound social changes, diligently sought to interpret the 'Revolution' in such terms. As explaining the events of the mid century came to be seen as the great task of seventeenth-century historians, researchers concentrated their efforts on the civil war and its antecedents. The post-Restoration period became unfashionable and, in the eyes of some, unimportant. The Revolution of 1688—9, once seen as the climactic event of the century, now appeared merely a confirmation of the great changes of 1640—60. To some, it was little more than a palace coup.

The last twenty years have seen a reaction against these trends. Historians have paid more attention to the later Stuart period as one worthy of study in its own right. Recent research on the 1680s has given new strength to the old belief that not all the great constitutional questions had been settled by 1660 and that there was a real possibility that some sort of absolutism might be established in England. Recent historians differ from their predecessors in avoiding moral judgments about such developments: there is little of the fervour and indignation of Macaulay or Ogg. The régimes of the 1680s are considered in functional terms: the main question is 'could they have worked', not 'were they evil'. This renewed interest in the later Stuarts has been strengthened by recent developments in the study of the civil war period. The confident socio-economic interpretations of the 1940s and 1950s have crumbled in the face of the awkward fact that whenever one tries to apply them in detail, they do not seem to fit: a series of excellent local studies have been especially important here. Disillusioned with attempts to explain the civil war as the outward manifestation of underlying social and economic changes, historians are taking a new look at the political events of the 1640s. They are coming to appreciate the importance of personalities, chance and the course of events in explaining why things happened as they did. All of this makes less plausible the earlier assumption that 1640–60 saw the culmination of a complex of great historical processes and that after 1660 nothing could be the same again. Perhaps the study of the origins of the civil war will not, after all, reveal all that is worth knowing about the seventeenth century. This makes it necessary to look once again at the events of 1688–9.

The importance of the Glorious Revolution was twofold: in what it prevented and what it brought about. Contemporaries were sure that James II wished to make himself absolute. Were they correct? It has been argued that Charles II and James II tried systematically during the 1680s to lay the foundations of an absolute monarchy (**116**). This, to me, is unconvincing, but there is no doubt that after the Exclusion Crisis England moved towards a more authoritarian régime. Until 1685 that régime rested on the consent and co-operation of a substantial section of the ruling élite and as such had every prospect of permanence. James's loss of Tory support forced him to rely more and more on his prerogatives, which served to confirm the Tories' latent suspicions that James's religion would oblige him to make himself absolute. There was, in fact, a great difference between James's intentions and his subjects' interpretation of his intentions, a fact which must be borne in mind in any assessment of his reign. Even if his subjects' interpretation was often wrong, however, it was shared by Whigs and Tories and helped bring about the Revolution. Attempts to explain the Revolution as a Williamite *putsch* (**95**) ignore the fact that William's invasion attracted minimal opposition and a great deal of enthusiastic support. If many Tories soon came to dislike William, very few were prepared to bring James back except on conditions which he showed no signs of accepting.

In considering the effects of the Revolution, we must distinguish between the intentions of the men of 1689 and what happened subsequently. Some historians have seen the members of the Convention as founding fathers, consciously creating a new constitutional order, acting out the dissolution and re-establishment of government on the lines laid down by Locke. This, it seems, was not the case. Most people were concerned with restoration rather than innovation, with patching up the old constitution and getting it working again. Any hopes of a radical renewal were frustrated by the need for a quick settlement which was acceptable to William and to Tories as well as Whigs. The settlement that emerged was ideologically obscure and untidy, but possessed the great, if negative, virtue of being totally unacceptable to very few. Pragmatism and ambiguity were the hallmarks of the Revolution settlement.

If the settlement was not revolutionary in itself, it marked the start of a period of rapid and profound changes. Some stemmed directly from the settlement. The Toleration Act effectively ended religious persecution in England. The refusal to grant William an adequate revenue initiated the decline of personal monarchy. Above all, William's arrival and James's flight to France forced England to join in the great war against France which had started in 1688. The scale of the military and financial effort required destroyed the last lingering vestiges of the crown's financial independence. It also had a profound impact on administration, finance and politics and made England a major European power, able to use her military and naval might to defend and extend her colonial empire. While the men of 1689 may have intended to end persecution and to vindicate the rule of law, these other developments were unforeseen and often unwelcome. Together they were to produce a nation whose society, political order and world role were very different in the eighteenth century from what they had been in the seventeenth.

John Miller

Part One: The Background

1   The Fall of James II

When James, Duke of York, was proclaimed king on 6 February 1685, few would have predicted that within four years he would be in exile in France, his departure regretted by hardly any of his subjects. Although the ports were closed and guards patrolled London's streets, there was no hint of disorder. Indeed, there were many spontaneous expressions of joy at the new king's accession.

The ease of his accession came as a surprise. Only a few years before, there had been a concerted attempt to exclude him from the succession to his brother's throne on the grounds that he was a Catholic. Three times between 1679 and 1681 the Commons had passed exclusion bills, but the Lords rejected one and the others were frustrated by Charles's dismissing Parliament. The Exclusion Crisis marked the climax of a growing mistrust between Charles and his parliaments dating back to the early 1670s. The peers and gentry who dominated Parliament had gladly welcomed Charles back in 1660 and had willingly restored an effective monarchy after the radicalism, disorders and military rule of the Interregnum, but they expected Charles to rule more responsibly than his father had done in the 1630s. During the 1670s they became concerned about Charles's friendship with France, whose military expansion in the Netherlands seemed to threaten England and whose king, Louis XIV, was the epitome of both absolutism and militant Catholicism. MPs also expressed anxiety about the 'growth of Popery' at home, partly because of Charles's ill-advised attempt to grant Catholics a modest toleration in 1672, but more because James, his heir-apparent, had become a Catholic (**90**).

In 1678 Titus Oates revealed an alleged 'Popish Plot' to assassinate Charles. Although his story was a pack of lies, few doubted its veracity and its implications were alarming. Hitherto the prospect of a Catholic king, although worrying, had been far from immediate. Charles was only three years older than James and in excellent health. If, as seemed likely, he outlived James, he would be succeeded by James's elder daughter Mary — and Mary and her husband, William of Orange, were Protestants. Oates's story forced people to consider what would have happened had Charles been killed. Experience taught that Catholic rulers persecuted their Protestant subjects with wanton and implacable cruelty, ignoring the constraints of humanity, morality and law. Catholic rule was identified with violence, armed force and illegality — in short, with 'arbitrary government', [**doc. 1**] the identification being emphasised by the conduct of Louis XIV. Although Oates declared that James was not involved in the Plot, he was the obvious beneficiary of the Papists' wicked schemes. To save themselves from the evils of absolutism and bloody persecution it seemed to a majority of the Commons and of the electorate that it was essential, a matter of self-preservation, to exclude James from the succession.

The exclusion campaign was the logical culmination of the Commons' growing distrust of both James and Charles. The outcome of the crisis was less predictable. Charles would not agree to exclusion, which he saw as the beginning of a wide-ranging attack on the rights and powers of the crown. In their efforts to overcome his resistance, the Exclusionists (or 'Whigs') tried to put pressure on him by mobilising mass support, using techniques of agitation and propaganda reminiscent of those of the Commons' leaders in 1641−2. As the panic of the plot died down, many peers and gentlemen who had been thoroughly unhappy about Charles and James's conduct in the 1670s came to see in the Whigs' tactics a threat to the established order in church and state far more dangerous than anything that James might do. As government propaganda stressed the parallels with 1641−2, more and more conservatives rallied to the king and his brother. The principles of these 'Tories' were summed up in the slogan 'Church and king'. They wished to maintain the ascendancy of the Church of England, against both Catholics and Protestant Dissenters, and to support the monarchy against the apparent threats of civil war and democracy.

The Tories' opposition to exclusion led the Whigs to denounce them as 'Papists in disguise'. The mutual recriminations and vituperation of Whig and Tory meant that by 1681 the ruling élite was more divided than at any time since 1660. Charles eagerly exploited this division. Frightened by the Whigs' behaviour, he threw the full weight of his authority behind the Tories. He dismissed Whigs from offices in local government and the militia and put Tories in their places. He encouraged the persecution of Dissenters, most of whom had supported Exclusion [**doc. 2**]. Above all, he used the law courts as instruments of political vengeance. Individual Whigs were prosecuted on charges of treason or on private suits and were condemned by Tory judges and Tory juries. In many boroughs the Tories sought a monopoly of local power by promoting an action of *quo warranto* ('by what right?') against the charter which conferred the borough's privileges and, often, laid down its form of government. The courts usually managed to find legal flaws in the charters. They were declared forfeit and new charters issued which gave the king extensive powers over the choice of municipal officials and members of the corporation. By these means the crown gained greater control than ever before over the boroughs' internal affairs. It would now be able to influence parliamentary elections in the boroughs, which returned the great majority of MPs. From 1684, in fact, it was the government, not the local Tories, who took the lead in initiating actions of *quo warranto* (**61, 75**) [**doc. 3**].

Thus in 1685, a few years after the monarchy seemed to be tottering, it had scattered its enemies – the Whigs were broken as a political force – and was on the verge of controlling elections. Parliament, it seemed, might become a 'rubber stamp', its membership determined by the crown like that of the French provincial estates. However, the crown had gained this power only with the Tories' co-operation and it could be exploited only if they continued to co-operate. Although the Whigs claimed that the Tories were unprincipled sycophants, who enlarged the king's power in return for places, the Tories had helped to build up the crown's authority for what seemed to them sound political reasons. The Whigs, they believed, were committed to rebellion and republicanism. Only a strong monarchy could prevent another period of political and social upheaval. James's assurances that he would uphold the Church's privileges and pre-eminence, and his defence of the episcopal church in Scotland, made them far less apprehensive than the Whigs about the prospect of James's becoming king. Even so, certain tacit conditions underlay their support for the crown's growing authority. So long as the king protected the Church, so long as he gave the Tories a monopoly of office, so long as he bent the law only against the Whigs, the Tories were quite content. If the king tried to use his newly-acquired powers against the Tories, their reaction would be very different.

James II and his subjects

James had much in common with the Tories. He had an exalted view of kingly authority and expected his subjects to obey him, but he also recognised that kings had a sacred obligation to care for their subjects' welfare and to rule according to law [**doc. 5**]. James differed from the Tories, and from the vast majority of his subjects, in being a Catholic. He became a Catholic in his mid thirties and his conversion was fully considered and psychologically satisfying. He thought in terms of black and white, right and wrong, and found in the Catholic Church an authority, a certainty, which (he felt) other churches lacked [**doc. 7**]. Like many converts, he wished to share his faith with others, but there were problems to be overcome. Catholic worship was forbidden by law. Catholics suffered various civil disabilities: they were excluded from Parliament and public office, so that Catholic peers and gentlemen were debarred from those positions of eminence to which their rank would otherwise have entitled them. Moreover, generations of Protestant preaching and propaganda had instilled strong prejudices against 'Popery' even if, in Defoe's words, people 'do not know whether it be a man or a horse'.

James faced formidable obstacles in his efforts to promote Catholicism, but he was determined to try. He hoped to find a Parliament that would repeal the penal laws (which forbade Catholic worship, education and publishing) and the Test Acts (which excluded Catholics from offices and from Parliament) [**doc. 8**]. He believed that once the Catholic clergy could compete with Protestants on equal terms, and once people could become Catholics without losing their chances of office, thousands of converts would come forward. He had no intention of imposing his religion by force: his army was predominantly Protestant and he expected to be succeeded by Mary. Not until late in 1687 was there a prospect that James's queen might give birth to a son, who would take precedence over Mary and be raised as a Catholic. Until then, James assumed that Mary would succeed him and firmly rejected suggestions that he should disinherit her in favour of a Catholic [**doc. 6**]. This meant that, in his efforts to have the penal laws and Test Acts repealed, he had to observe the forms of law, as any violence against the Protestants would be repaid, against the Catholics, after his death. As the Marquis of Halifax acutely noted (**8**):

> Converts will not venture till they have such a law to secure them as hath no exception to it; so that an irregularity, or any degree of violence to the law, would so entirely take away the effect of it that men would as little run the hazard of changing their religion after the making it as before.

James's strategy thus depended on his persuading a parliament to repeal the penal laws and Test Acts. This would require the co-operation of at least a section of his subjects. England in 1685 was still a mainly agricultural country, its values and politics dominated by the owners of land, the nobility and gentry. Those who made their fortunes elsewhere — in the law and civil service, the colonial trades or banking — mostly bought country estates and sought to merge into the landed élite. This élite had dominated local government since time out of mind, except during the much execrated Interregnum. It controlled most parliamentary constituencies, boroughs as well as counties, and provided the great majority of MPs. James therefore needed the co-operation of at least part of this élite to carry his programme through parliament, so its attitude towards James and towards Catholicism was crucially important.

Unfortunately for James, Tories and Whigs, Anglicans and Dissenters, agreed in detesting Popery, if in little else. The Tories had rallied to James in the Exclusion Crisis despite his religion, because they feared that the Whigs would start a civil war. Both Tories and Whigs were against allowing Catholics freedom of worship. Those few who might allow them toleration were against their being admitted to offices or to Parliament: once in power, they believed, Catholics would maltreat and persecute Protestants. 'I can with a very good conscience', wrote the Tory Earl of Clarendon in 1688, 'give all liberty and ease to tender consciences...but I cannot, in conscience, give those men leave...to come into employments in the state who by their mistaken consciences are bound to destroy the religion I profess' (**49**). As for James, although the Tories had given him the benefit of the doubt, they still watched warily for signs that he might abuse his power and become another Louis XIV. Most Tories took it for granted that Catholicism and absolutism went hand in hand. James might be convinced of the purity of his intentions; he might believe that he acted only according to the law of God and the law of the land, and might dismiss his subjects' suspicions as absurd or malicious; but those suspicions, however ill-founded, were a fact of political life. Given English Protestants' preconceptions about the malign political implications of Popery, it was not surprising that James's subjects placed the worst possible construction on his conduct. James was to give them ample cause to do so.

The course of the reign

In 1685 the obvious strategy for James was to rely on his 'old friends', the Tories. He promised to maintain the Church's dominant position and continued to persecute Dissenters. This strategy was vindicated when a general election produced an overwhelmingly Tory House of Commons. This voted James the revenues enjoyed by Charles and additional sums to pay some of the crown's debts, refit the fleet and crush the rebellion led by Charles's bastard son, the Duke of Monmouth. Monmouth's defeat seemed to signal the final destruction of Whiggery. The reprisals which followed, the Bloody Assizes, may seem abhorrent to modern eyes but aroused little protest among the Tories (**40**) [**doc. 4**]. The rising gave James a pretext to double the size of his army. In future, he could feel more secure against rebellion or invasion.

Unfortunately for James, events in 1685 showed not only the bankruptcy of Whiggery but the limits to the Tories' enthusiasm for him. While prepared to vote him an adequate revenue and to support him against Monmouth and his radical followers, the Commons would do nothing to benefit the Catholics. In November both Houses expressed concern about James's enlarging the army and his commissioning eighty to ninety Catholic officers, in defiance of the Test Acts. Standing armies were always seen as instruments of absolutism and James's conduct seemed doubly sinister at a time when Louis XIV was using his army to convert Huguenots to Catholicism. Incensed by what he saw as its groundless suspicion and insubordination, James prorogued what was probably the most co-operative and exuberantly monarchist parliament of the century. It never met again.

The Tory Parliament's conduct forced James to rethink his position. If the Tories would not co-operate in repealing the penal laws and Test Acts, James would have, first, to change his strategy and, second, to resort to more dubious methods. On the first point, he would have to abandon the Tories and seek support elsewhere, among the Whigs and, more particularly, the Dissenters. If an Anglican Parliament refused to grant relief to Catholics, a Dissenting Parliament might grant a general toleration from which both Catholics and Dissenters would benefit. To appeal to the Dissenters required a certain psychological adjustment on his part. Although personally tolerant of individual Dissenters, James's experience (and that of his father) led him to equate religious dissent with political sedition: 'It must needs be faction and not religion if men could not be content to meet five besides their own family, which the law dispenses with' (the Conventicle Act applied only to meetings of more than five persons). However, as he became more angry that the Anglicans had turned against him, so he convinced himself that most Dissenters had been driven into sedition only by religious persecution. By the end of 1686 James was ready to stake all on an appeal to the Dissenters and confident that his appeal would succeed.

Appealing to the Dissenters raised several problems. Like Catholics, Dissenters were unable to worship freely and suffered various legal disabilities: their exclusion (in principle) from municipal office could prove a particularly serious blow to James's plans for a parliament, as the great majority of constituencies were boroughs. Since 1680−1 the crown had sought to harass the Dissenters and break their political influence, putting power firmly into Tory hands. If there was to be any chance of a Dissenting Parliament, the Tories' stranglehold on power in the localities had to be broken and that of the Dissenters built up: indeed, it had to be built up further than their lowly economic and social status warranted. James's plans could succeed, therefore, only if the Dissenters were freed from their disabilities *before* the laws against Dissent were legally repealed and if their local political influence was artificially enhanced. At the same time, James wished to encourage conversions to Catholicism and to allow the small Catholic minority to add its limited weight to the campaign for repeal. In order to achieve these objectives, however, James had to use methods which involved dubiously legal extensions of the prerogative and which, given his subjects' preconceptions, were bound to provoke fears that he planned to establish absolutism.

The extensions of royal authority were of two types. The first involved the dispensing and suspending powers. Nobody denied that the king possessed a power of pardon or that in certain cases he could dispense individuals from the penalties of the law 'where equity requireth a moderation to be had'. He was expected, however, to use such powers sparingly, inquiring fully into the merits of each case. When Charles II suspended the laws against religious nonconformity in 1672, the Commons told him that this was illegal, but there was no statutory restriction on the king's use of his dispensing power. James considered it monstrously unjust that he should be deprived of the services of his Catholic subjects, so thought it quite proper to allow them, on his own authority, to hold offices, dispensing them from the penalties of the Test Acts. In June

1686, in the test case *Godden v. Hales*, the judges ruled that the king possessed a dispensing power and could decide when it was necessary to use it [**doc. 9**]. Many of James's subjects were unimpressed by the judges' ruling, partly because James had dismissed those judges who thought differently (**60**) but more because of what followed. Although it was easy to dispense individual office-holders from complying with the Test Acts, it was impossible to issue individual dispensations to the thousands of Dissenters and Catholics who wished to worship freely — free from the penalties laid down by law. In April 1687, therefore, James in effect dispensed the whole nation from complying with the penal laws, pending their repeal by Parliament. He thus moved from selective dispensations to the wholesale, if temporary, suspension of a body of laws. This suspending power was legally far more dubious than the dispensing power: statutes could be abrogated only if repealed by Parliament. It was made to appear doubly sinister by the suspicions already aroused by James's religion. If he could suspend the penal laws, might he not try to suspend all laws? If he did, nobody's person or property would be safe [**doc. 10**].

The second extension of royal authority came in the campaign to pack parliament. To break the Tories' electoral influence and build up that of the Dissenters, James revived and extended the methods of 1681–5. Tory municipal officials and JPs were replaced by Dissenters (or Catholics); more borough charters were confiscated and new ones issued. In addition, various pressures were brought to bear on electors and possible candidates. In the winter of 1686–7 James had interviewed MPs from his first Parliament in a last effort to overcome their opposition to repealing the penal laws and Test Acts. Having dissolved that Parliament in July 1687, James ordered the JPs be tendered the 'Three Questions', which required them to state their position on repeal. Those who declared their opposition were dismissed and replaced by others whom James hoped would prove more tractable. Given the Tory gentry's dominance in the counties, and the wide franchise, James stood little chance of success in the shire elections, so the main thrust of his electoral campaign was in the boroughs. There the electorate was often very small and the franchise disputable, which gave ample scope for gerrymandering, fraud and intimidation. Some corporations were purged several times until James was confident that he had found men to do his bidding. In one, the electorate was allegedly reduced to three, of whom two would elect the third. At Huntingdon it was proposed to enrol soldiers as electors; elsewhere army officers were named as candidates. Such manipulation was backed up by canvassing and propaganda. As James wished especially to win Dissenters' support, many of his agents and canvassers were Dissenters, who had (ironically) learned their trade working for the Exclusionist Whigs (**73, 75**) [**doc. 11, 12**].

Both the extension of the dispensing power and the campaign to pack Parliament were inspired by what were (in James's eyes) the purest of motives and merely extended prerogatives and techniques which had previously attracted little criticism. It was the extension of the king's powers beyond traditional limits and the suspicion aroused by his religion which made James's conduct appear so threatening. If by such means James could secure a House of Commons dominated by persons as inconsiderable, atypical and unpopular as the Dissenters, Parliament would cease to be representative of the dominant elements in English society. It might then become a mere rubber stamp for royal policies. Moreover, once the Test Acts were repealed and Catholics could enter Parliament, similar methods might produce a Papist Parliament which could pass laws against Protestantism. As with the extension of the dispensing power, James's campaign to pack Parliament might have a limited objective – the repeal of the penal laws and Test Acts – but its wider implications were alarming. Together James's actions seemed to threaten to destroy both the laws and the independence of Parliament, the very foundations of the traditional constitution.

As James needed a Dissenting Parliament to repeal the penal laws and Test Acts, the Dissenters' reaction to his approaches was crucial. On one hand, his offer of full toleration and free admission to office was very attractive after a generation of persecution and harassment. Most Dissenters took advantage of James's Declaration of Indulgence to worship openly, but when it came to supporting the repeal of the Test Acts, many had grave reservations. Most Dissenters were strongly anti-Catholic and feared that, once in power, Catholics would seek to destroy Protestantism. Anyway, the Test Acts affected them far less than the Catholics. The Dissenters were thus subjected to conflicting pressures. The king's agents argued that they could make sure of the liberty they now enjoyed only if they repealed the Test Acts as well as the penal laws. They claimed that Dissenters had nothing to fear from the Catholics and that they should be happy to repeal the Test Acts, as a gesture of gratitude to James. James's opponents appealed to anti-Catholic prejudice, arguing that the indulgence was designed only to give Catholics the power to impose their religion by force. The bishops, until recently advocates of persecuting Dissenters, now appealed for Protestant unity and approached some of the moderate Dissenters with proposals for a more broadly based national church. Perhaps most telling was the pamphlet *A Letter Written by Mijn Heer Fagel*, disseminated in large numbers early in 1688. As long as Mary was James's heir presumptive, her attitude (and William's) to the question of repeal was crucial. James tried hard to persuade them to support repeal publicly, but while they were ready to agree to toleration, even for Catholics, they refused to consider the repeal of the Test Acts [**doc. 15**]. This was stated authoritatively in Fagel's *Letter*, which thus thwarted the attempts of James's propagandists to play on Dissenters' fears that toleration would end when James died. The *Letter* showed that William and Mary would continue it, so the Dissenters did not need to pay James's price – the repeal of the Test Acts – for their future liberty [**doc. 13**].

By the summer of 1688 it seemed clear that James had alienated the Anglicans without winning over the Dissenters [**doc. 14**]. This was shown when seven bishops petitioned against an order that the Anglican clergy should read the Declaration of Indulgence in their churches, which would give the impression that the Church endorsed it. The bishops were imprisoned on a charge of seditious libel, but were visited in gaol by leading Dissenters, and their acquittal was greeted with a wave of rejoicing which the government could neither prevent nor punish. Meanwhile, there was every sign that the campaign to pack Parliament was failing. James delayed holding a general election and eventually called one only as a panic measure, in the face of imminent invasion; he recalled the writs when it became clear that the gesture had done nothing to regain his subjects' support (**89**). But if James's policies were failing and his regime was widely unpopular, it was by no means on the verge of collapse. Inertia and habits of obedience to authority made rebellion unlikely, especially as the Bloody Assizes had served as a reminder of what happened to unsuccessful rebels. The king had an army of twenty thousand which, although mainly Protestant, seemed loyal. The English nobility had long since ceased to keep private armies, and the gentry showed little inclination for war. James's regime could be challenged only by a professional army and that could come only from outside the British Isles. The immediate causes of James's downfall must therefore be sought abroad, in the Dutch Republic.

Invasion

William III's position in the Republic was a peculiar one. The Republic was a federation of seven provinces, of which Holland was much the richest and most influential. The federation's constitution placed great emphasis on the rights and autonomy of individual provinces and, within each province, those of the major towns. Such a decentralized system was ill suited to providing decisive leadership, in diplomacy or war. For that, the Republic traditionally looked to its greatest family, the House of Orange. The princes of Orange held various important offices but their power also stemmed from their prestige, as a quasi-royal family, and the individual princes' ability to exploit the complexities of the Republic's political system. There was a continual tension between the provinces' traditions of local autonomy and the efforts of successive princes to establish an effective centralised régime, partly for its own sake, partly to enable them to make war more effectively. The provinces and towns accused the princes (especially William III) of seeking to become absolute monarchs; the princes accused their opponents of parochial selfishness, corruption and bloody-minded obstruction (**59**).

In 1685 William's foreign policy was hamstrung by the long-standing opposition of Amsterdam and the other great towns of Holland. William was convinced that Louis XIV wished to conquer the whole of the Low Countries as the first stage of a plan to dominate all Western Europe. He was also convinced that Louis wished to eradicate Protestantism. His opponents believed that the threat from France was less serious than William claimed and that he exaggerated the danger of war as a pretext to raise an army, which could make him absolute at home. For much of the 1680s they denied him the money and the army he needed for an effective foreign policy. In order to explain the Revolution of 1688, therefore, one must examine not only William's conduct but also the dramatic change in Dutch public opinion between 1685 and 1688.

William's understanding of James's conduct was, if anything, more distorted than that of the English. He believed that republicanism was far more powerful in England than it really was: he was a grandson of Charles I, and James had repeatedly told him that the Exclusion Crisis was a republican plot against the monarchy and royal family. Moreover, most of the English and Scots in the Republic were political or religious exiles, including some republicans. Much of William's information about English

11

affairs came from such people (notably Gilbert Burnet), which helps explain why he accepted stories which were exaggerated or untrue and overestimated the extent and extremism of the opposition to James's policies within England [**doc. 16**]. Small wonder, then, that he feared that James might provoke another civil war which, if it led (like the last) to a republic, would frustrate his wife's claim to the throne and ruin his chances of bringing England into the next war against France, which he saw as inevitable [**doc. 15**].

It was not only the danger of a republican uprising which seemed to jeopardise Mary's right to succeed her father. There were rumours that James might alter the succession in favour of a Catholic — perhaps his illegitimate son, the Duke of Berwick. James denied any such intention [**doc. 6**] but William's anxieties remained. Late in 1687 came a more serious threat: it was announced that James's queen was pregnant. His Catholic courtiers, with more optimism than political sense, proclaimed their confidence that she would produce a son, who would take precedence over Mary in the succession. Suspicious Protestants, who believed the Papists would stick at nothing, expressed doubts as to whether she really was pregnant and remarked cynically that, whether she was or not, the Jesuits would doubtless arrange for a boy to appear. This expectation that a spurious child would be passed off as the queen's legitimate offspring underlay William's decision, late in April 1688, to invade England 'if he was invited by some men of the best interest to ... come and rescue the nation and the religion' (**2**). The invitation was signed by only seven men, mostly not of the first rank politically, but it provided a measure of formal justification for a decision that William had already taken (**78**). The signatories assured William that the vast majority of people wanted a change and that James's army would not fight. The birth of James's son on 10 June merely confirmed William's decision. Protestants seized on every supposedly suspicious circumstance of the birth to support the claim that a monstrous fraud had been perpetrated. The most popular story was that a baby had been smuggled into the queen's bedchamber in a warming-pan. Behind such stories lay a fervent wish that James should have no Catholic heir and they were given credence by the fatuous over-confidence of some Catholics. 'Nothing is more evident' wrote one of William's correspondents in England 'than that a trick was designed, otherwise they would not have acted like mad people in making the thing disputable, but if they really put the thing in execution or not, God knows.... Be it a true child or not, the people will never believe it.' Whatever the English believed, however, events were increasingly determined by what happened on the continent.

Since 1685 more and more Dutch people had come to share William's obsessive fear of French attack. The revocation of the Edict of Nantes, the maltreatment of Dutch merchants in France and the influx of Huguenot refugees all helped to revive a dormant sense of Protestant solidarity. Prohibitive new French tariffs damaged Dutch trade to a point where, in commercial terms, the Dutch had nothing to lose from war with France. Meanwhile, Dutchmen were increasingly anxious about James's domestic policies and his apparent friendship with France. If he became absolute and imposed Catholicism at home, he would be better able to join the French in attacking the Dutch (as Charles had done in 1672). James was not, in fact, allied to France, but his tactless and inconsistent policy towards William and the Dutch (plus his Catholicism) led many to believe that such an alliance existed and that, sooner or later, James and Louis would mount a Catholic crusade against the Republic. Given such a belief, a pre-emptive strike (to prevent England from joining with France) seemed very desirable, but it would surely be dangerous to denude the Republic of troops when Louis might attack at any time. This danger was removed when Louis, fearful of the revival of Habsburg power in Germany, sought to strengthen his eastern frontier by seizing Philippsburg. The attack escalated into a major war, tying down Louis's armies well away from the Dutch frontier and leaving William free to prepare to invade England.

William took great risks in deciding to invade. Not for some months was he sure that the French would be occupied elsewhere; even then, it was possible that Louis might attack the Republic before William's forces could get back. His army of around fourteen thousand was much smaller than James's, so he relied heavily on the assurances he received that James's men would not fight. Above all, it was foolhardy to begin a major naval expedition against the prevailing wind at the onset of winter: indeed, when William's fleet first set sail, it was driven back by a storm. In order to justify such risks, the rewards of success would have to be very great. James's followers claimed later that William aimed from the outset to seize the crown, a claim echoed by some historians (**95**). William no doubt considered the possibility of becoming king, but the evidence suggests that he would have been satisfied with less. His declaration to the English recounted the misdeeds of James's government,

13

demanded an inquiry into the birth of his son and referred all matters to a free Parliament [**doc. 17**]. (William had been reluctant to put himself at the mercy of a body as unpredictable as a parliament, but his English allies had insisted that without this he would win no support.) It seems that his minimum aims were to secure Mary's claim to the succession (by having James's son declared 'supposititious') and to secure a free Parliament which, he assumed, would force James to declare war on France and perhaps give William some say in the conduct of that war. With England in the war and the succession secure, William could wait for James to die, whereupon he would gain full control of England's resources in his great struggle against France.

The good fortune attending William was never more apparent than when the wind veered to the east, driving his fleet down the Channel and bottling James's up in the Thames estuary. Devout Protestants saw in this evidence of divine favour, a belief strengthened by William's landing at Torbay on 5 November, the anniversary of another deliverance from Popish malice. Having landed, time was on William's side; disillusionment with James was bound to work in William's favour. When James became aware of the danger of invasion, he had thrown over the Dissenters and appealed again to his 'old friends', the Tories, but they showed little eagerness to defend him in his hour of need. They were piqued at losing their offices — 'Some would think one kick of the breech enough for a gentleman' — and took at face value William's declaration that he came to secure a free parliament, which they saw as the best cure for the nation's ills. Having been restored to their local offices, the Tories expected to do well in a general election and then to shape a settlement which would prevent James from abusing his power in future, while avoiding any change of ruler or other radical alterations. Tory militia officers found various pretexts not to oppose William's forces, while bishops and Tory peers urged James to call a free general election and so remove any pretext for William and his army to remain in England.

James, however, refused to put himself at his subjects' mercy. He argued that there could be no free election while a foreign army remained in England. He preferred to rely on his army, swollen by newly-raised regiments and others brought from Ireland and Scotland. James's army was much larger than William's, even after he had left several regiments to keep order in London, where simmering resentment at the opening of Catholic chapels had finally broken out into violence. It was, however, far from easy to find and engage William's army, since the roads were rendered almost impassable by winter rain and frost. Moreover, even if James could come to grips with the enemy, there were worrying signs of disaffection within his army. Most of the soldiers were Protestants, who resented the bringing over of Irish Catholic troops and who shared the political prejudices and anxieties of their civilian counterparts. As James marched westwards, several units deserted, together with certain officers (notably James's nephew, Lord Cornbury, and his protégé, Lord Churchill) from whom he had especial reason to expect total loyalty (**34**). Convinced by these defections that he could not rely on his army, and perturbed by the news that in the North many nobles and gentlemen had appeared in arms against him, James retreated to London and began to negotiate. The conditions which William offered were not unduly harsh. They envisaged James's remaining king, with reduced powers, which would suggest that William was not determined to seize the throne [**doc. 18**]. James, however, had negotiated only in order to buy time. He was determined to accept no terms, however reasonable. Having sent his wife and son off to France, he slipped away from Whitehall on the night of 10 December and headed for the Kent coast.

James decided to flee partly because he feared for his safety but also because, if a 'free parliament' met, he would have to agree to an inquiry which would lead to his son's being branded as spurious: "Tis my son they aim at and 'tis my son I must endeavour to preserve, whatever becomes of me.' By fleeing he avoided unpalatable concessions and, in theory, reserved his position, but his flight was bungled through a mixture of incompetence and ill-luck. Apprehended by a group of fishermen, who thought he was a Jesuit, James was brought back to London on the 15th. His flight had disconcerted the Tories, who thought it cowardly and irresponsible. He had made no provision for government to continue and had seemed to go out of his way to cause confusion. He destroyed the writs drawn up for a general election and (apparently) had the Great Seal thrown in the Thames. Worst of all, he ordered his generals to disband their men without any provision for disarming them first. This could have caused chaos, had not most of the officers maintained discipline among their men and submitted to William. Such conduct encouraged some Whigs to argue that James had shown himself unfit to govern and had forfeited his right to the crown. As it was, London saw two days of serious anti-Catholic rioting, while the provinces were convulsed with rumours that the

Irish were coming to murder and pillage.

William's reaction to James's flight was one of quiet satisfaction. James had clearly left of his own volition: nobody could accuse William of driving him out. He might well have taken the advice of some of his followers and declared himself king, had not James's escape been prevented. William was clearly annoyed by this; now he had to exert more obvious pressure to make James leave. In the middle of the night Dutch troops replaced the English guards at Whitehall. James was woken up by William's emissaries, who advised him to leave London 'for his own safety'. James asked to go to Rochester. William agreed and on the 18th James left London by river, with a guard of Dutch soldiers, which made it clear that he was leaving under duress. This enabled Tories later to forget the ignominy of James's first flight and to argue that William had driven him out by force. James's Tory friends begged him not to go, but he was bent on flight and William had no intention of placing obstacles in his way. On the night of the 22nd he slipped out of a back door which William deliberately left unguarded. He landed in France on Christmas morning. Meanwhile, separate assemblies of peers and of former members of the Commons invited William to take over the conduct of government, for the time being, and to issue letters of summons for a general election for a 'Convention', to meet on 22 January 1689. At last the 'free parliament' which William had demanded was to meet, but without the king who should have summoned it.

Part Two: The Revolution Settlement

2 The Change of Ruler

At the start of 1689 William was performing many of the functions of a king. He commanded the armed forces (both James's and his own) and directed the civil government. Logic and common sense suggested that his position should be regularised by his being made king. His mother had been a Stuart and he was married to James's daughter. His being recognised as king, however, raised complex problems of political principle and political calculation. The divisions between Whig and Tory, so deep in the early 1680s, had been obscured by their common alarm at James's conduct. The question of who was to be the monarch revived the emotive differences about the succession and the nature of monarchy which had divided the nation during the Exclusion Crisis.

The Whigs argued, both in the Exclusion Crisis and in 1689, that monarchy was a human institution which existed for the benefit of its subjects. Its function was to dispense justice and protect the subject against violence at home and attack from abroad. This implied that if a monarch misused his powers, or threatened to do so, he should have his powers restricted or, in the last resort, he should be removed. In the Exclusion Crisis, the Whigs argued that James's Catholicism made it virtually certain that he would abuse his powers if he became king. It was thus a matter of national self-preservation to exclude him from the succession. The logic of the Whig approach was weakened by their unwillingness to develop the full implications of their ideas. They were inhibited partly by innate conservatism, but more by the traumatic effect of the events of 1640–60 on the ruling élite. Those accused of Royalism had had their lands confiscated without due process of law, an attack on the sanctity of property which perturbed many non-Royalists. Families which had directed county affairs for generations were elbowed out by militants, upstarts, even soldiers. In 1660 the gentry, Royalist and Parliamentarian, united to restore the old order. The Exclusionist leaders (who included men, like Essex, of impeccably Royalist antecedents) had to tread a delicate middle path, to pressurise Charles into agreeing to exclusion without provoking another civil war. They tried to create an impression of popular insistence on exclusion while confining their agitation to peaceful and lawful channels (**90**). They argued that Charles should act on the Commons' advice, but were vague about what would happen if he did not. They talked of Edward II and Richard II, who came to sticky ends after ignoring their subjects' wishes. This implied that subjects had a right to resist their king, but arguments from the right of resistance had been discredited by Charles I's execution and were not explicitly used in the Exclusion Crisis (**23, 87**).

Although the Exclusionists' arguments had been theoretically untidy, the events of 1688 strengthened and simplified their position. William succeeded where three parliaments had failed: James was excluded without his subjects seriously sullying their hands with rebellion: most of the risings of November and December were supposedly intended to protect Protestants against violence from the Catholics (**79**). Thus the Whigs were willing, indeed eager, to accept William as king. Most of them believed in monarchy and thought that, if William became king, he would be able to prevent James's return. With their functional, utilitarian view of monarchy they had no qualms about altering the strict line of succession: some more radical Whigs thought it would be easier to curtail the power of a king with a weak title. Whigs of all shades of opinion urged that William should be made king — and hoped, in return, for a monopoly of office. They had, they believed, been in the political wilderness for far too long.

If the Whigs welcomed James's departure, the Tories' feelings were very mixed. They had defended James's interests in the Exclusion Crisis partly because they feared civil war, but also because they were genuinely attached to the hereditary principle. In their alarm and anger they had laid greater stress than before on the sanctity of royal authority and on the subject's duty not to resist his king. Reassured by James's promises to respect the law and protect the Church, they had joined with the king to crush the Whigs. James's behaviour as king came as a nasty shock. Tory gentlemen watched with fear and incomprehension as James bullied the Anglican clergy, bent the law and replaced Tory office-holders with Papists and Dissenters. William's arrival and his promises of a free parliament seemed providential. Few Tories showed any inclination to resist the invader, even if some were unhappy that their fellow-countrymen were appearing in arms against their king. 'How these risings and associations can be justified I see not,' wrote Sir John Bramston, 'but yet it is very apparent had not the Prince come and these persons thus appeared, our religion had been rooted out.'

James's Tory friends urged him to concede William's demand for a free parliament. This would remove any pretext for William's demanding more, and there was the further advantage that a Tory Parliament could force James to restore and maintain the Tories' monopoly of office, while reversing his measures in favour of Catholicism. James's flight upset their plans. They now saw that by failing to oppose William they had made possible James's expulsion. Their hopes of regaining power and bringing James to heel evaporated. William seemed more friendly to Whigs and Dissenters than to Tories and Anglicans. Some Tories may have felt guilty at having helped drive James out, however unintentionally, but their guilt was soon subsumed in anger at William's having duped them. On 1 January Sir Edward Seymour told Clarendon (**4**) that

> all honest men were startled at the manner of the king's being sent from Whitehall; that all the West went in to the Prince of Orange on his declaration, thinking in a free parliament to redress all that was amiss; but that men now began to think that the Prince aimed at something else; and that the countenance he gave the Dissenters gave too much cause of jealousy to the Church of England; who, he said, were the most considerable and substantial body of the nation.

Thus while the Whigs were in favour of making William king, the Tories were against it, partly because it would violate the hereditary succession, partly because they felt that William had tricked them into betraying their principles. Much therefore depended on the outcome of the elections to the Convention. William ostentatiously withdrew the troops under his command from the parliamentary boroughs. In some there was confusion as to which charter was in force, but in general the elections were peaceful. Although the party allegiances of the new MPs were not always apparent, it seems clear that a majority of the new House of Commons were Whigs (**68, 96**). The Lords, thanks in particular to the bishops, had a Tory majority. Thus agreement could be reached only if the Houses were willing to compromise or if one of them bowed to outside pressure.

There were five possible ways of settling the succession. The first, to invite James back, was soon ruled out. Tories as well as Whigs had found his government intolerable and his decision to desert his kingdom rather than negotiate suggested that he would be most unlikely to agree to any reasonable conditions. A second possibility was for William to be sole monarch. William liked this idea, but his

English supporters did not. Admiral Herbert, who commanded the invasion fleet, said that he would not have done so had he known William could behave so badly towards his wife, while the Tories would never agree to an arrangement which made William's conquest of England so obvious. Most Tories, indeed, wished to preserve James's right to the crown and to avoid tampering with the succession, so proposed making William and Mary regents for James. They argued that James had forfeited only his right to exercise the powers of the crown, not his title. Against this, the Whigs (and a few dissident Tories) claimed that it was impractical to separate the exercise of royal power from the title to it and that if James was not deprived of his title he might choose to return. The regency proposal was heavily defeated in the Commons and rejected by three votes in the Lords.

This left two possibilities. After the failure of the regency proposal, the Tory majority in the Lords claimed that, with James's departure, the crown had passed to Mary as next heir. This would prevent James's return and do as much to maintain the hereditary principle as was possible in the circumstances. It ignored James's son, but many Tories regarded him as spurious. To emphasise his exclusion, the Lords concurred with a Commons' resolution that it was unsafe for a Protestant kingdom to be ruled by a Popish prince. It would also remove any need for Parliament to meddle with the succession and thus salve the consciences of the Tories who, during the Exclusion crisis, had argued that the hereditary principle was sacred and unalterable. The Commons, however, refused to adopt this solution. A majority of MPs was clearly in favour of the fifth possible solution – offering the crown jointly to William and Mary. Such a dual monarchy would be exceptional and could not easily be reconciled with the theory of a hereditary succession. So abnormal an arrangement could not be made by any authority other than Parliament and many MPs were glad of this and wanted the offer of the crown to come explicitly from Parliament, because they wished to lay down the conditons upon which that offer should be made. 'Before the question be put, who shall be set upon the throne,' said Lord Falkland, 'I would consider what powers we ought to give the crown, to satisfy them that sent us hither' (**7**). Making William and Mary king and queen would also give some recognition of the risks which William had run and the expense he had incurred, as well as satisfying MPs' prejudices concerning the proper relationship of husband and wife. In the words of Henry Pollexfen, if Mary 'be now proclaimed queen, can anything be more desirable than that her husband be joined with her in the government?... Does any think the Prince of Orange will come in to be a subject to his own wife in England? This is not possible, nor ought to be in nature' (**7**).

Thus the Lords argued that Mary was already queen, the Commons that the Convention should offer the crown jointly to William and Mary. The two Houses sought to resolve their differences in a conference on 6 February. To complicate matters, the conference was ostensibly concerned, not with the succession, but with what had happened to James. The Commons had resolved on 28 January

> That King James II, having endeavoured to subvert the constitution of the kingdom, by breaking the original contract between king and people; and by the advice of Jesuits and other wicked persons having violated the fundamental laws; and having withdrawn himself out of this kingdom; has abdicated the government; and that the throne is thereby vacant.

The Lords objected to the word 'abdicated', preferring the more neutral term 'deserted', and also to the suggestion that the throne was vacant, which implied that the Convention had the right to fill it [**doc. 22**]. The debate ranged around these points, but the Lords' underlying concern was clearly to prevent William's being made king (**88**). It was William who resolved the deadlock. At each stage he had been careful to act apparently at the behest of the English. He had demanded an invitation before preparing to invade, he had come to London only when invited by the City authorities and he had hoped for an unsolicited invitation to become king. The Lords' obstruction annoyed him. A quick settlement was essential. Some of James's old regiments were mutinous and the Protestant minority in Ireland was being overrun by the Catholics. The longer a settlement was delayed, the greater were the fears that radicals and republicans might profit from the confusion. William therefore summoned some leading peers and told them that he would not act as regent, nor would he be subordinate to his wife. As a mere consort, he would lack a clearly defined position. More important, his authority would lapse if his wife died before him (as Philip II's had on the death of Mary Tudor). Thus if the Lords would not agree with the Commons to make him king on his own terms, he would go home and leave the English to extricate themselves from the ensuing confusion. To sweeten the pill, he agreed that Mary's sister Anne and her children should succeed before any children he might have by a later marriage [**doc. 19**]. Faced with William's firm stand, the Lords'

21

resolution crumbled. Some Tory peers slipped away and Halifax, the Speaker, pushed through a resolution concurring with that of the Commons. The Lords then resolved that the crown should be offered jointly to William and Mary. The next week was spent in waiting for Mary to come from Holland and in completing the list of 'conditions' upon which the crown should be offered (which became the Declaration of Rights). On 13 February the crown was offered formally to William and Mary, who were then read the Declaration, now expanded to include the arrangements for the succession which William had proposed and a new oath of allegiance. The crown was to pass as if James were dead (ignoring his allegedly spurious son), first to Mary and her heirs, then to Anne and her heirs and finally to any heirs which William might have by a later marriage. Thus the Convention tried to maintain the hereditary principle as far as was possible. James was declared to have forfeited his right and William was joined with his wife in an unprecedented dual monarchy, but when it came to the *transmission* of the right to the throne, the Convention had adhered closely to the hereditary principle, the right being passed on first by Mary, then by Anne, and finally by William.

3 The Significance of the Change of Ruler

Later generations regarded the change of ruler in 1689 as being very significant, but tended to interpret what happened in those few days in the Convention with the dubious benefits of hindsight, so that what really happened became obscured by myth and misunderstanding. Much of this misunderstanding stemmed from the publication, barely a year after the event, of Locke's *Two Treatises of Government*. Locke's avowed purpose was to justify the Revolution and his *Second Treatise* seemed to provide a logical and lucid analysis of what had happened.

Locke claimed that men were rational beings, who formed themselves into political societies for their individual and collective good. Such societies made possible the creation of a framework of laws to resolve disputes — about property, for example — which in a state of nature could be settled only by force. Political societies were formed by a voluntary 'original compact', whereby men agreed to abandon some of the rights and liberty they had previously enjoyed and to submit to a common set of laws. This original consent was renewed, tacitly, as each new generation grew up to enjoy the protection of the laws. The laws were amended, or extended, by a legislature entrusted with that task by the people. They were enforced by an executive, which should ideally be part of the legislature but should not dominate it, since the combination of legislative and executive powers in the hands of one man, or a few men, was likely to lead to tyranny. If such tyranny arose, the government was dissolved. The people were absolved from their duty to obey it and could set up another in its place [**doc. 21**].

In considering the usefulness of the *Two Treatises* in understanding the Revolution, one should ask, first, whether they marked a new departure in English political and constitutional thought and, second, how far Locke's account of the dissolution and re-constitution of government fitted the facts of 1689. On the first point, there was much in Locke that was unfamiliar. Seventeenth-century Englishmen normally thought of the constitution and of political relationships in terms of law and history — as the common law relied so heavily on case law and precedent, the two were closely related. The constitution was seen as an organic growth, dating back beyond the days of written records and enshrining the wisdom of untold generations. Nobody could tell when the laws, or the powers of the king, or the rights of the subject had originated, but they were seen as having grown up in a symbiotic relationship and could best be defined by means of precedents. Such an historical approach could pose problems. Precedents were of little help in dealing with unprecedented circumstances, like those of 1641–2. They could also prove embarrassing. Historical research was challenging the assumption that Parliament was as old as the monarchy. If, as it now seemed, the monarch had brought Parliament into being, could he not also dispense with it? If William I had arbitrarily imposed new laws on England after the Conquest, could not later kings, equally arbitrarily, revoke those laws or impose new ones? Some claimed that it was not only unhistorical but also illogical to suggest that laws could evolve, as it were, independently. Some authority – presumably a king – must have enacted and enforced those laws. In other words, absolute monarchy was a more natural and logical form of government than limited monarchy. Despite such problems, the will to believe in the ancient constitution was immensely strong. Faced with unpalatable facts or arguments, men ignored them or took refuge in obscurantism. None the less, by 1688 the concept of the ancient constitution was somewhat battered, especially after the Tory onslaught of 1680–85 (**99, 107**).

Locke did not invent the idea that monarchy should be limited or that kings should rule in the interests of their people. Such beliefs were central to the theory and practice of the ancient constitution: English kings, for instance, were unable to impose taxes or promulgate laws without the consent of their subjects in Parliament. Locke parted company from the mainstream of English constitutional thought by abandoning the argument from English history. He used illustrations from antiquity or the Old Testament, but his system drew its force not from historical examples but from a theoretical argument about the origins of government and of political society. In this, he had much in common with Hobbes (hardly a 'mainstream' figure) but their presuppositions and conclusions were very different. Both agreed that governments were essentially artificial constructs – no one form was inherently superior to others, or had the stamp of divine approval. Both saw government in utilitarian terms: it had to serve a practical purpose, not enforce any particular set of values. But whereas Hobbes saw men as violent and irrational, Locke saw them as rational and wise. Whereas Hobbes saw the task of government as protecting men from violence, Locke saw it as protecting property and the right to a peaceful and prosperous existence. Whereas Hobbes argued that government needed despotic power to perform its functions properly, Locke argued that its power should be limited. Finally, whereas Hobbes argued that submission to government should be absolute and unconditional so long as its protection continued, for Locke submission was always conditional on the government's fulfilling its responsibilities, which (as mentioned earlier) extended well beyond mere physical protection.

Although Locke differed from most Whigs in abandoning the argument from history, the thrust of his argument was similar to that of the Exclusionists; indeed, he wrote most of the *Two Treatises* during the Exclusion Crisis. Locke, however, developed to the full those implications of the Exclusionists' arguments which they had been reluctant to draw. They had talked mainly of the king's moral obligation to govern in his people's best interests and, more particularly, to follow the Commons' advice. Talk of such an obligation might imply that there was some sort of contract between ruler and ruled, but there is almost no mention of 'contract' or 'compact' in the surviving records of the parliamentary debates of Charles II's reign. The concept of contract was familiar enough in law, but seems rarely to have been used in constitutional discussions before 1689, perhaps because of the obsession with arguments from history. It should be made clear that Locke did not talk of a contract between ruler and ruled. His 'original compact' occurred when a political society was formed. When the members of that society established a government they did so, not by a 'contract', but in the form of a 'trust'. A contract gave the ruler rights and obligations. A trust imposed upon him only obligations. His power was vested in him in order to serve particular ends. If he failed to achieve those ends, the trust could be terminated [**doc. 21**].

With the concept of a trust, Locke gave theoretical form to the old belief that a ruler should rule in his subjects' interests. Traditionally, that view had often been expressed using the analogy of 'patriarchal' authority: a father would, by the law of nature, do what was best for his children. This analogy implied that a king's authority over his people was like a father's over his family — inherent in his position and thus unquestionable, part of the natural order of things. Locke was inspired to write the *Two Treatises* by the publication of Filmer's extreme restatement of the patriarchal view. Locke denied that anybody exercised authority as of right: it had to be vested in them by the political community as a whole. The concept of a trust also left open the possibility that authority could be taken away if it was not used for the purpose for which it had been given. The criteria for taking back this authority were not objective (the breach of certain fixed rules) but subjective — the people believed that the ruler was not ruling as he should. Moreover, it was up to the people as a whole to decide when this occurred — in other words, when their ruler was ceasing to act for their good and degenerating into a tyrant. When that happened all obligations of obedience were dissolved and the people could resist him — by force if necessary — remove him and establish what government they chose in his place [**doc. 21**].

In this Locke moved well beyond the norms of Whig thought. Whigs might agree that people were justified in defending their homes against robbers or against Catholic soldiers, enlisted contrary to law, but memories of civil war and the natural conservatism of property-owners made most Whigs reluctant to endorse the right of resistance in any but the most restricted cases. They certainly were not prepared to grant it to the people in general, as Locke did, or to allow the people in general to set up what form of government they chose. If that were permitted, what would happen to the ancient constitution? Locke argued that experience suggested that people would not move against the government except under the most extreme provocation and that, if the government were to be re-established, it would probably be very much along traditional lines. Even so, his theory smacked unpleasantly of anarchy to many moderate Whigs. Whereas for Locke sovereignty lay in the people, for most Whigs it lay in parliament, in the ancient trinity of king, Lords and Commons. This concept had tradition behind it, but begged the question of what to do if one of the three elements was missing, as in 1689, or if the three could not agree among themselves, as in 1642 or in 1679—81.

Locke, then, took familiar, often semi-developed concepts and expressed them in an abstract theoretical form at variance with the normal concrete, historical ways of thinking of the ancient constitution. He also developed his arguments far beyond the point which most Whigs regarded as safe or desirable. They wished to be freed from the dangers of 'Popery and arbitrary government', not to give ordinary people the power to overthrow established authority or to refashion the constitution. As a result Locke's influence was limited in the generation after 1689. Most Whigs still argued from history or took the Revolution itself as the starting-point of a new constitutional order.

This brings us to the question of how far Locke's *Two Treatises* described what actually happened in 1688–9. In a sense, one should not expect them to. Locke's insistence on arguing in general terms, his use of subjective criteria of acceptability and his avoidance of arguments from English law and history make the *Treatises* very unspecific. It is hard to see anything directly relating to England in the discussion of the origins of government, but the same is not true when Locke discusses how governments can be dissolved. The hypothetical constitution which he considers closely resembles that of England, with a king and bicameral legislature. Also several of the ways in which he says a government can be dissolved could refer directly to James II: for example, through a king setting his will above the laws or tampering with elections. How far, then, can James's removal be seen in Lockean terms?

First, the question of a 'trust'. The Convention's debates contain few references to the monarch's power being a 'trust' from the people, but there are many references to a 'compact' or 'original contract'. The Commons' resolution of 28 January referred to James's 'breaking the original contract between king and people'. However, most of those who used the phrase were very vague as to what it meant. A few saw it as an historical event, the very beginning of government. Others saw it as the exchange of oaths, whereby the king swore at his coronation to rule according to law and the people swore an oath of allegiance. Most, however, used the term so vaguely that one cannot tell what they understood by it. Its appearance in 1689 perhaps represents an attempt to articulate a sense of betrayal, felt by Tories as well as Whigs. They believed that James had failed to fulfil his obligations to his people and did not wish him to remain their king. The use of the concept of 'contract' offered one way of expressing both their disgust at his mis-government and the feeling that this absolved them from their obligations to him. If the term was much used, it does not, however, seem to have been clearly understood. On 29 January the Lords summoned a group of lawyers and asked them what the original contract was. Sir Robert Atkyns replied

> I believe none of us have it in our books or cases; not anything that touches on it. Thinks it must refer to the first original of government. Thinks the king never took any government but there was an agreement between king and people. It is a limited

monarchy and a body politic and the king head of it. If there were an original contract yet it is subject to variations as the times.

Sir Edward Nevill put his thoughts more succinctly: 'It must of necessity be implied by the nature of government' (**88**) [**doc. 24**]. It is therefore doubtful whether the men of 1689, despite the language they used, had a Lockean view of the original contract, or of a ruler's trust, in any but the most embryonic form. At most, the idea of 'contract' provided a way of expressing the feeling that James had forfeited his right to rule. Was he therefore deposed for breaking the original contract? A quick reading of the resolution of 28 January might suggest that he was, but the Commons concluded that he had 'abdicated the government'. The resolution as a whole is ambiguous. One could argue that the 'abdication' followed directly from James's 'having withdrawn himself out of the kingdom', with the remaining clauses, about contract and the fundamental laws, being merely illustrative. One could also argue that James's breaches of the law and of the original contract were as much part of his abdication as was his leaving the country: they were all part of the process whereby he proclaimed his unfitness to rule. To explain this ambiguity we must consider the circumstances of the Convention. Locke was one man writing a work of theory. The Convention was a large and politically divided body struggling with the practical problem of settling the succession before William went home in disgust or the country collapsed into anarchy or republicanism. There were many Whigs in the Commons who doubtless believed that James had forfeited his right to rule and ought to be deposed: Jack Howe said in 1694: 'I was for deposing King James and setting up King William' (**7**). There might just have been enough who felt that way to have secured a majority in the Commons in favour of deposition, but such a resolution would never have passed the Lords. For many Whigs the really important thing was to remove James and put William and Mary in his place. As long as that happened, the precise form of James's removal was comparatively unimportant. Some Whigs, moreover, probably doubted whether Parliament had the right to depose a king.

For these reasons the question of deposing James never really arose. The Whigs chose to argue that he had abdicated, thus placing the blame where they believed it belonged. The Tories might have been expected to welcome this argument, as a way of getting rid of James without deposing him. In fact, they showed distinct reservations about it. Even after the rejection of a regency, some still argued that James had forfeited only the exercise of kingly power, not his right to be king. Some complained that the term 'abdication' was unknown to English law. (The Whigs replied tartly that the same was true of 'desertion', the term the Tories preferred.) Some who saw the abdication solely in terms of James's withdrawal claimed that he had been driven out by William's troops. Above all, the Tories resented the linking of the abdication with the alleged vacancy of the throne. If the throne was vacant, it implied that Parliament could fill it, but since the Exclusion Crisis the Tories had asserted vehemently that Parliament could *not* determine the succession. Moreover, only if Parliament could fill the throne could it offer it jointly to William and Mary, and the Tories were determined to keep William out, if they could. They therefore claimed that the throne was not vacant, although the Lords refused to say who actually occupied it.

However, if (as they claimed) the crown could pass only by the normal method of descent, it could pass only to Mary. The Tories therefore insisted that for Parliament to fill the throne would make the monarchy elective, a claim which the Whigs vehemently denied.

The arguments about the finer shades of meaning of 'abdication' and 'desertion' are far removed from the Lockean view of a people deposing their ruler if he betrayed his trust. Two other Lockean concepts must also be considered: the right of resistance and the dissolution of government. When William came over with an army and various aristocrats rose against James, it might seem obvious that they were engaging in resistance to their king, but few admitted this. Those who assembled at Nottingham on 22 November 1688 declared: 'We own it rebellion to resist a king that governs by law, but he was always accounted a tyrant that made his will his law; and to resist such an one we justly esteem no rebellion, but a necessary defence' (**79**) — sentiments which Locke certainly shared. Lord Wharton told the Commons that he had helped to drive James out and would willingly do so again. In general, however, such arguments seemed both unnecessary (since the main emphasis was on James's abdication, not his deposition) and dangerous: with the country, it seemed, teetering on the brink of anarchy, it must have seemed most unwise to avow openly the people's right to resist their rulers.

For much the same reasons there was little talk of the dissolution of government. Lady Mordaunt wrote to Locke that there was 'an occasion not only of mending the government but of melting it down and making all new' (**12**). Interestingly, Locke did not agree. He wrote on 29 January: 'The settlement of the nation upon the sure grounds of peace and security is put into their [the Convention's] hands, which can no way so well be done as by restoring our ancien government, the best possibly that ever was, if taken and put together all of a piece in its original constitution.' Lord Wharton, while prepared to justify having resisted James, said that, when it came to settling the government, 'I hope it will be done as near the ancient government as can be' (**7**). Although one or two anxious Tories took pains to argue that the government had not been dissolved, hardly any of the Whigs suggested that it had been. They, like the Tories, believed in the ancient constitution. James's abdication, they argued, left a void at the top of the structure of government, but otherwise it remained essentially unchanged. 'The constitution, notwithstanding the vacancy, is the same,' said Sir John Maynard, 'the laws that are the foundations and rules of that constitution are the same' (**14**). The void, or vacancy, had been created by James, not by the people. The task of the people, or rather its representatives, was to fill it. This was a matter not of ideology, but of pragmatism. James had left them without a government, so they had the choice between perpetual anarchy or providing for themselves [**doc. 23**].

For these reasons it is misleading to see the Revolution as a triumph for Whig ideology — if one interprets 'Whig ideology' in a Lockean sense. If anybody showed a stubborn attachment to ideology in 1689 it was the Tories. They argued inflexibly that for Parliament to determine the succession would destroy hereditary monarchy and make the crown elective [**doc. 22**]. Beneath this inflexibility lay not only an obstinate determination to prevent William from becoming king, but also a real commitment to principle. Since the Exclusion Crisis, the Tories had developed a powerful and coherent ideology based on the exaltation of royal power, the sanctity of the hereditary principle and the subject's duty not to resist lawful authority. It was an authoritarian ideology, well suited to a party whose leaders were born to a position of social eminence and whose Church was hierarchically organised, with authority flowing down from the top. It seemed especially appropriate at a time of renewed fears of civil war and social upheaval. Whereas there was some tension between the Whigs' social conservatism and their sporadic demagogy, the Tories' political and social outlooks blended naturally together. In general, indeed, the Tories' ideology was more coherent and fully developed than that of the Whigs. Its great flaw was the assumption that the king would respect the law, protect the Church and rely on Tory support. As long as he did so, the Tories' exaltation of royal authority made sound political sense. James's unexpected behaviour left the Tories confused and bitter. A minority, like Danby, opposed him openly. Most found themselves left behind by events, with little choice but to acquiesce in a change of ruler which they had not wanted. A few (most of them clergymen) refused to swear allegiance to William and Mary and lost their places. Most salved their consciences by recognizing the new rulers as *de facto* and not *de jure* monarchs, which was made easier by the omission of 'rightful and lawful' from the new oath of allegiance [**doc. 47**].

While most Tories were prepared, sooner or later, to swallow all the oaths that were tendered to them, there is no doubt that many suffered severe qualms of conscience. Their emotional attachment to monarchy may seem strange to modern eyes, but it was genuine and did not end in 1689. Despite the gloomy prophecies of elective monarchy, there was every reason to expect that the infringement of the hereditary principle would be only temporary. Once James and William were dead, the succession would flow back into its proper channel and all would continue as if nothing had happened. Such expectations, however, were frustrated by the death of Anne's last surviving child, the Duke of Gloucester, in 1700. Mary had died without children in 1694 and William showed no inclination to remarry, so it was clear that the Protestant Stuart line would end with Anne. This left a choice between James's son, the 'Old Pretender', who was being raised as a Catholic in France, or the nearest Protestant relative, Sophia, Electress of Hanover, who was descended from James I's daughter. In 1689 Anne's prodigious fecundity seemed to offer the certain prospect of a Protestant Stuart dynasty, which meant that the Tories would not, in the long run, have to choose between Protestantism and legitimism. After Gloucester's death, however, the Tories had to face that choice. They plumped for Protestantism, for Hanover, but with an ill-disguised reluctance, expressed not only in a marked lack of enthusiasm for their future foreign ruler but also in a last doomed wallow in divine-right emotionalism under Anne.

The Revolution had not killed the Tories' belief in divine right any more than it had killed their belief in hereditary monarchy. If the Tories had not continued to take the sacred attributes of monarchy so seriously, they would not have made such difficulties about recognizing William's title to the throne. Their truculent and aggressive behaviour towards William reflected, not an abandonment of their reverence for monarchy, but their conviction that William was not a proper monarch. With Anne's accession the Tory veneration for monarchy resurfaced effusively. (This did not, incidentally, prevent Tory politicians from trying, almost as ruthlessly as the Whigs, to force their wishes on the queen.) Tory pulpits rang again with the rhetoric of non-resistance. The practice of touching for the king's evil, suspended under William, was revived for the last time. It was George I's accession, not William's, that finally killed off belief in divine right. In 1689 the Tories could look forward to the day when Anne would became queen. In 1714, their fatuous hopes that the Pretender might turn Protestant were soon dashed, after which there was no future for the Anglican legitimism which had been the backbone of Toryism. It was not so much the events of 1688–9 as Queen Anne's gynaecological problems which destroyed the Tories' attachment to hereditary monarchy and divine right.

If the change of ruler in 1688–9 marked neither the triumph of Locke's view of the constitution, nor a defeat for Tory ideology, what was its significance in the history of ideas? It did of course inspire Locke to publish the work he had written almost a decade earlier. It was also a victory for a Whig view of the constitution more modest and untheoretical than that of Locke. The generation after 1689 saw only a limited development of the theory of contract, which still tended to be equated with the ancient constitution [**doc. 24**]. It also saw a continued use of the claim that England's was a mixed and balanced constitution, with an increasing emphasis on the separation of powers [**doc. 25**]. The Whigs' constitutional ideas, however, remained rudimentary and intellectually undistinguished. Their approach to the constitution was dominated by pragmatism. In 1689 they did not bother their heads overmuch about the origins of political authority or whether the Convention, which had not been summoned by a king, could act as a parliament. They were ready to adopt the fiction of James's abdication, which enabled them to remove him from the throne without deposing him. When asked what authority they had to name his successor, they appealed to common sense and the right of self-preservation. If they did not fill the throne, chaos would follow. They did not see this as a precedent: a situation so extraordinary could hardly be expected to arise again. They avoided awkward questions about fine points of legal propriety and concentrated upon what needed to be done to patch up the old constitution and get it working again. Their arguments rested on vague concepts of expediency and the public good [**doc. 23**]. These concepts, used earlier by the Exclusionists, could be found in Locke, but for most Whigs Parliament (not the people as a whole) was to decide what was in the public interest. Such nebulous guiding principles could lead to flexibility, inconsistency, even cynicism. It is hard to think of any principle embraced by part or all of the Whig party in the 1690s which had not been betrayed by at least some of its leaders by 1720. After 1689 the days of the Tories' attachment to ideology and religion were numbered. The future lay with the Whigs and with the politics of pragmatism, expediency and cynicism (**80**).

4   The Constitutional Settlement

On 28 January the Commons resolved that James had abdicated and that the throne was vacant. Next day a committee was appointed to 'bring in general heads of such things as are absolutely necessary to be considered for the better securing our religion, laws and liberties'. 'Before any person was named to fill the throne', wrote Sir John Reresby, 'they would frame conditions upon which only he should be accepted as king and tie him up more strictly to the observance of them than other princes had been before' (**15**). This reflected, not a desire to limit the monarch's powers for the sake of it, but bitter experience of the Stuarts. 'Because King Charles II was called home by the Convention and nothing settled, you found the consequence', said Sir William Williams (**7**). On 2 February the committee brought in a list of twenty-eight heads. The House noted that some merely reaffirmed existing rights and laws, whereas others would change the laws and so require legislation. It therefore ordered the committee to separate the two elements. The committee reported back on the 7th, with its recommendations now divided into two sections [**doc. 26**]. The first, declaratory section contained twelve heads, all of which had appeared in the first list; a general reference to parliament's privileges now became a specific claim to freedom of speech and of debate. The second section listed twenty heads on which legislation was needed. Several points appeared in both sections — for example, the need for free elections and frequent parliaments. Two of the original heads had disappeared from the list — the provisions that no pardon could be pleaded to an impeachment and that parliament should remain in session until all necessary business had been completed.

The committee reported on the afternoon of the 7th. That morning the Commons heard that the Lords had concurred with their resolution of 28 January and had voted to offer the crown to William and Mary. The Lords also sent down a new oath of allegiance, without the phrase 'rightful and lawful'. It was proposed that the Commons should join in this offer of the crown, but after some debate it was resolved to consider the committee's report first.

Most of those who advocated this order of proceeding were Whigs, but it was a Tory, Sir Robert Sawyer, who proposed an addition to the second section (approved by the House) that Catholics be excluded from the throne. The debate resumed next day. A committee now recommended that the first section of the heads (the restatement of existing rights) should be joined to the Lords' votes on the offer of the crown and the new oath of allegiance, while the second section should be dropped. Despite some opposition, this proposal was adopted. The Commons concurred in the vote to offer the crown to William and Mary, agreed to the new oath of allegiance and sent these up to the Lords, together with the statement of rights and proposals on the order which the succession should follow after William and Mary. The Lords agreed next day to the provisions for the succession, but disagreed with the wording of some of the heads in the statement of rights. They disliked the unequivocal condemnation of the dispensing power which, if properly used, could be useful to the subject. The Commons agreed to add the rider 'as it hath been assumed and exercised of late' and to omit the last phrase from the provision that parliaments 'ought to be held frequently and suffered to sit'. The Commons were also persuaded to add the phrase 'as allowed by law' to the statement of the right of Protestants to keep arms for their own defence: clearly the peers feared that this might otherwise tend towards 'arming the mob'. The differences between the Houses were settled on the 12th and on the 13th the whole package was read to William and Mary, after the offer of the crown.

The most mysterious element in this chain of events was the decision to drop the second part of the list of rights and grievances. This has been explained in various ways, but two explanations seem plausible. William's supporters in the Commons, men like Sir Robert Howard and Sir Richard Temple, urged the House to concentrate on restating known rights. This would avoid the controversy, and the inevitable delay, involved in a more elaborate and innovatory programme. In support of this contention, one could point out that few of the proposed measures ever became law, but it is also worth noting that the list of heads was merely a declaration of intent, not a legislative enactment. Even so, it is clear that the more novel and controversial the document was, the easier it would be for those bent on trouble to use it as a pretext for delay. If the Lords objected to some of the comparatively conventional provisions of the first section, they would have made far more difficulty about accepting the more novel proposals in the second. The other decisive factor was, yet again, the attitude of William. He clearly disliked some elements of even the modified document and considered vetoing it when it was made into a bill. William denied having made known, informally, that he was against the novel restrictions in the original document, but many believed that this was his opinion and that those who advocated such restrictions were unlikely to enjoy his favour. It would have been typical of William to seek to influence events by making his feelings known in this indirect manner (**52, 69**).

If it is not clear why the Declaration of Rights ended up in its eventual form, the Declaration's legal status is even less clear. The concern shown by both Houses and by William about its wording and contents would suggest that it was seen as containing conditions which William and Mary had to accept before ascending the throne. However, this was not made explicit and William did not promise to abide by the terms of the Declaration. Instead, he told the Houses 'as I had no other intention in coming hither than to preserve your religion, laws and liberties, so you may be sure that I shall endeavour to support them'. One could thus see the Declaration as being purely for the new monarchs' information. It told how Charles and James had abused their powers, with the implication that William and Mary should avoid such abuses; in no sense was it an explicit formal contract between ruler and ruled. This was tacitly recognised later in 1689, when the Declaration was turned into a bill, which would not have seemed necessary had it been regarded as an unequivocal contract. The first Bill of Rights was lost by prorogation after a series of disputes between the Houses. The second passed with little difficulty. As eventually passed, the Bill differed from the Declaration in including an absolute prohibition of dispensations (except where specifically allowed by statute) and a clause debarring any Catholic, or the wife or husband of a Catholic, from becoming king or queen of England. Although both Houses had passed resolutions to this effect in January and such a provision had been added to the ill-fated second section of the heads of grievances, this became law only with the Bill of Rights and remains so to this day.

When William gave his royal assent to the Bill of Rights, he at last bound himself formally to adhere to the terms of the Declaration read to him almost a year before. But how far did these terms impose novel and effective limitations on the crown? Most referred to specific abuses of royal prerogatives during the 1680s, but did not call into question the prerogatives themselves. The suspending power was declared illegal and the dispensing power severely restricted, which, given James's stretching of a judgement in favour of the dispensing power, is hardly surprising. Some clauses referred as much to Charles's reign as to James's — for example, the assertion of the right of petitioning or the condemnation of abuses of the legal system. Several declared that parliament should meet frequently and that elections and debates should be free — sentiments which were conventional enough and which reflected resentment at recent attempts to intimidate MPs and tamper with elections. Perhaps the only real novelty was the statement 'that the raising or keeping a standing army within the kingdom in time of peace, unless it be with consent of parliament, is against law'. The army's legal position had long been uncertain. Charles II was the first king to possess a standing army, usually referred to by the euphemistic title of 'guards and garrisons'. It was not large and was dispersed in numerous garrisons, at home and abroad. Only when he raised additional land forces for war, notably in 1673 and 1678, did Parliament express serious anxieties about the danger of military rule. Charles's parliaments consistently refused to provide for a larger army: they had had enough of military rule under Cromwell and saw a large standing army as synonymous with absolutism. Common lawyers, too, were reluctant to acknowledge the army's existence. They did not regard mutiny and desertion as crimes and would not recognise the courts martial which the crown set up to punish these offences. After James's great expansion of the army, which raised acute fears of absolutism, such indeterminacy could no longer be tolerated. The Bill of Rights made it clear that the king could not legitimately keep up any permanent land forces without parliament's explicit approval: tacit connivance was no longer sufficient. Moreover, the Mutiny Act of 1689 allowed the punishment of mutiny and desertion by martial law for only a limited period; henceforth, a new Mutiny Act was passed each year. Thus at any time parliament could revoke the right to hold courts martial simply by failing to pass a new act.

By these means parliament asserted its control over the maintenance of military discipline and over the army's very existence. The clause relating to the army was, however, the only novelty among the Bill of Rights' constitutional provisions. The remainder were largely restatements of what most people regarded as the constitution. Some were general to the point of vagueness — for instance the assertion that 'Election of Members of Parliament ought to be free'. How was one to define 'free'? Even if one could

define it, the Bill made no provision for ensuring that elections were
in fact free. It was simply a series of statements of principle, often in
nebulous terms. Moreover, it contained no mechanism for its own
enforcement. And yet the Bill of Rights came to be seen as an
outstanding constitutional document, almost on a par with Magna
Carta. As early as 1690, one MP called it 'our original contract'. It
influenced the framers of the United States Constitution: the
assertion of the 'right to bear arms' and the prohibition of 'cruel and
unusual punishments' both became amendments to that
constitution. In explaining this apparent anomaly, we must look
beyond the terms of the Bill itself. If the limitations on the
monarchy which it outlined did, in fact, become established, along
with many others, this owed little to the amiable generalities of the
Bill. The main reason must be sought in the changed relationship of
crown and parliament, which had its origins not in any specifically
constitutional changes but in the Revolution financial settlement.

5 The Financial Settlement

From the start, some MPs in the Convention clearly saw the royal finances as the key to any settlement. The Convention of 1660 had assessed the crown's annual expenditure as £1,200,000 (including the army and navy). Charles was granted a number of revenues, notably the customs, excise and hearth tax, which were (optimistically) expected to yield that amount. In the 1660s the yield fell lamentably short, but in the 1670s and 1680s it improved greatly, thanks to a boom in overseas trade (**41**) and more efficient administration. Charles had, at first, reverted to the old practice of tax farming. A group of financiers would undertake to collect (say) the customs, paying the king a fixed annual rent and keeping all they collected in excess of that rent. This had the advantage of ensuring prompt and regular revenue payments, while the farmers proved a valuable source of loans to a government whose credit was never strong. Its great disadvantage was that, if trade expanded rapidly, the farmers profited rather than the crown. By 1685 tax farming had been abandoned and all three major branches of the revenue were being collected directly, by salaried officials. The yield of the ordinary revenue had grown to around £1,500,000 a year, sufficient to enable Charles to survive without Parliament. James II's Parliament granted him the same revenues, without enquiring into their current yield (**32**).

It seems probable that the parliaments of the early 1660s had intended not to make Charles financially independent but to provide just enough for the ordinary expenses of government so that, if he needed more, he would have to ask parliament. They returned in principle to the tradition that the king should 'live of his own', that he should normally subsist on revenues enjoyed in perpetuity or granted for life, but they were careful not to give so much that he would have no need of parliaments. The main difference was that before the civil wars much crown revenue had come from land and feudal rights, which the king enjoyed as his own property. After 1660 all the crown's major revenues were granted by parliament. Even so, the basic distinction was maintained between ordinary revenue (granted for life or forever, to cover normal expenditure) and extraordinary revenue (voted for a limited period, for wars or other emergencies).

When Charles II complained that his ordinary revenue was inadequate, the Commons voted him extraordinary supplies rather than increase his ordinary revenue. Despite such precautions, however, Charles ended up able to live without Parliament. The men of 1689 were determined not to make the same mistake. On 29 January William Sacheverell told the Commons: 'Secure this House, that parliaments be duly chosen and not kicked out at pleasure; which never could have been done without such an extravagant revenue that they might never stand in need of Parliaments.' To William Harbord, the financial settlement was the crucial question. 'You have an infallible security for the administration of the government. All the revenue is in your own hands, which fell with the last king, and you may keep that back. Can he whom you place on the throne support the government without the revenue?' (**7**). On 26 February the Convention, which had now declared itself a full parliament, debated the revenue. Whigs like Birch and Pulteney joined with Tories like Clarges and Seymour to urge that William be granted the revenue for no longer than three years [**doc. 27**]. It was eventually decided to investigate the revenue's current yield before coming to any decision.

The Convention's approach continued dilatory. William tried to buy the Commons' co-operation by offering to give up the unpopular hearth-tax, which had been granted to the crown in perpetuity. The Commons accepted his offer, but extended the customs for three months only. In the words of Sir William Williams 'If you give the crown too little you may add at any time, if once you give too much, you will never have it back again' (**7**). On 20 March the Commons resolved to settle on the king a revenue of £1,200,000 a year, but this figure was arrived at arbitrarily, without investigation of the king's needs, and was insufficient to support the crown even in peacetime. Now that the king had to send military aid to the Irish Protestants and was soon to make war against France, it was totally inadequate. Moreover, the Commons soon decided that half this figure would suffice for the civil administration (a gross underestimate), so that the other £600,000 could go towards the war. The Commons then deducted this amount from the figure for extraordinary supply (itself far less than was needed), so that by the autumn of 1689 the king was forced to borrow on the credit of future revenues and so was sucked into a vortex of debt. To add insult to injury, the Commons made no permanent provision for the revenue (although they extended the customs for another six months). William offered to produce accounts to show that nothing was being wasted and that he was desperately short of money. His offers were brushed aside with claims that the Commons lacked the time to go through detailed accounts and wild allegations of embezzlement and overspending.

William, never the most patient of men, was furious. He 'said the Commons used him like a dog. Their coarse usage boiled so upon his stomach that he could not hinder himself from breaking out sometimes against them' (9) [doc. 28].The enforced consensus of the early days of the Convention was over. Tories like Clarges vented their spleen on the man they saw as a usurper. Many Whigs were angry that William had denied them the monopoly of office which they had expected; they especially resented his employing Nottingham, who had argued in February that the throne was not vacant. Many backbenchers simply thought that they were being asked to vote too much in taxes. To make matters worse, the Whigs devoted more energy to paying off scores against the Tories than to doing the king's business. By the beginning of 1690, William had had enough. He dissolved the Convention and called a new parliament − which in due course settled the revenue, but hardly to William's satisfaction.

The settlement was thrashed out in an atmosphere of party rancour, complicated by allegations of gross financial mismanagement which made the Commons less willing than ever to grant the ordinary revenue for life. William was voted the customs until 1694 (later extended to 1699 and then 1706). He was also given the temporary part of the excise for life: the remainder, being perpetual, he collected anyway. He was thus the first king since the fifteenth century (with the somewhat peculiar exception of Charles I) not to be granted the customs for life. Even if they had been granted for life, his ordinary revenue would have been much less than James II's. He had lost the hearth money and the French war diminished the yield of the customs. James's ordinary revenue averaged around £1,500,000; William's seldom yielded more than a million, sometimes less (69, 100, 102). Moreover, so much of the ordinary revenue was applied to the war and it became so encumbered with debts that it was harder and harder to separate it from the extraordinary supplies voted specifically for the war. Thus by 1698 the excise (intended mainly for the support of the civil government) was £600,000 in debt and half the customs revenue was appropriated for the navy. The war had thus destroyed the last traces of the idea that the ordinary revenue was an independent income for the king. In 1695—6 the Commons recognised this by arranging to borrow £515,000 for the civil expenditure, or civil list, and in 1697 they voted a supply of £515,000 for the same purpose. In 1698 William was voted a number of revenues for life, designed to bring in £700,000 a year, which was to cover the civil list: any surplus was to be applied to public purposes. It says much for the inadequacy of William's existing resources that he was delighted with this arrangement (**100**).

Having distinguished at an early stage between the civil and military elements in the crown's ordinary expenditure, the Commons had increasingly taken over responsibility for military and naval expenditure as a whole, voting money to pay the interest on debts incurred on the various branches of the ordinary revenue. Under the pressures of war, the old distinction between ordinary and extraordinary revenue became so blurred as to be meaningless. It was superseded by a more realistic distinction between civil and military revenue. Such a distinction seemed particularly necessary in 1697—8, when many were unwilling to trust William with the army left over from the war, but it would probably have developed anyway. With the king given a revenue adequate only for his civil expenditure, the tradition that he should 'live of his own', which had received some mortal blows in 1689—90, was buried forever. From the reign of Anne, the monarch was voted the civil list for life, while the army and navy estimates were put before Parliament each year (**69, 100**).

The failure to grant William an adequate revenue in 1689—90 was quite deliberate (**102**). 'If you settle such a revenue as that the king should have no need of a Parliament', said Paul Foley, 'I think we do not our duty to them that sent us hither.' 'Granting it for life will prevent any ill ministers from being called in question', declared Colonel Austen (**7**). Dislike or distrust of William made the Commons determined not to surrender the financial weapon placed in their hands by the Revolution. The issue was not purely one of curbing the king's power, but also one of investigating and punishing the misdeeds of his ministers. Whatever the motives, the destruction of all hopes of an independent royal revenue transformed the crown's relationship with parliament. Now the Commons, if they chose, could in theory force their wishes on the king, simply by withholding supply. In practice, as we shall see, the picture was much more complex, but the fact remains that the great constitutional change brought about by the Revolution owed far more to the impact of the financial settlement (compounded by the war) than to the change of ruler or the Bill of Rights.

6 The Religious Settlement

In 1640 there had been one Church in England to which everybody except Catholics nominally belonged, although there was much disagreement about what sort of church it should be. By 1660 the problem of the nature of the national church had been joined by another, the treatment of the growing number who did not want to be part of that Church. On the nature of the Church, there were two broad streams of opinion. The first, the older one, could be labelled Puritan, or Low Church, or (more hesitantly) Presbyterian. It harked back to the days of Elizabeth and James I, when the Church's theology had been Calvinist, when its clergy placed more emphasis on preaching the Gospel than on formal observance and when many parish ministers ignored official requirements such as wearing a surplice or using the sign of the cross in baptism. The second stream could be called Anglican (although the term was rarely used), or Arminian or Laudian (after Archbishop Laud) or High Church. This came to prominence in the 1620s. It marked a reaction against the Reformation, an attempt to restore elements of the pre-Reformation church which some came to see as valuable. Whereas Low Churchmen believed that there were too many 'popish' practices left in the Church, High Churchmen argued that some of what was called 'popery' served a valid liturgical or spiritual purpose. High Churchmen wanted a visually impressive service; they believed that communion should not take second place to the sermon; their theology, influenced by Arminianism, tempered the stark predestinarianism of Calvin with a revived emphasis on free will; and they saw the priest as spiritually distinct from and superior to his flock, his task to direct and order their spiritual lives.

This divergence of views on the nature of the Church was a major cause of the civil war. Resentment of Laudian innovation and the need for Scottish support induced the Long Parliament to abolish bishops, but most English Presbyterians (unlike their Scottish counterparts) had no dogmatic hostility to episcopacy. Their ideal remained the Church of Elizabeth and James I. They were willing to be members of an episcopal church, provided it was purged of

Laudian innovations (although memories of Laud and his colleagues made them seek to limit episcopal power by associating representatives of the parish clergy with the bishops in the Church's government). In 1660 Anglicans and Presbyterians were arguing, much as in 1640, about the nature of the national church. However, since 1640 there had emerged many congregations which did not want to be part of any national church. These 'gathered churches' paid no heed to parish boundaries and, unlike the Church of England, they were spiritually exclusive: only 'visible saints', who could show evidence of conversion and spiritual purity, were welcome. Whereas Anglicans and Presbyterians agreed that the Church should embrace sinners as well as saints, and try to redeem them, the gathered churches, buoyed up by hopes of an imminent Second Coming and Day of Judgement, saw no need to concern themselves with those who were soon to be consigned to hell-fire. They were to bring together the few who would be saved and seek God together. Originally very varied and loosely organised, by 1660 most congregations belonged to a specific sect — Independent (or Congregationalist), Baptist or Quaker.

The new sects did not have vast numbers of adherents, especially among the ruling élite, but their supporters were too numerous for talk of a single English Church to be anything more now than a pious fiction. Both in 1660 and in 1689, there were two problems to be faced. First, should the Church's liturgy and government be adapted to make them more palatable to Presbyterians? Should a real effort be made to comprehend both the older 'Puritan' tradition and the newer Laudianism within a single church? Should ministers be allowed some latitude on such matters as wearing the surplice? Should bishops share their authority with the inferior clergy? Second, should the Church recognise that part of the population no longer wished to belong to any church which mixed sinners with saints? Should it allow toleration to the sects, or use the apparatus and penalties of law in an effort to force them into conformity?

At the Restoration the answer to both questions was a firm 'no'. Charles favoured comprehension and toleration but the firmly Anglican House of Commons elected in 1661 did not. It prevented any concession to the Presbyterians and passed a series of Acts against non-Anglicans (now known as Dissenters or Nonconformists). Not only could they not worship freely, but they were debarred from politics and public office and became second-class citizens. Although the ruling élite had shown little enthusiasm for Laudianism in 1640, much had changed since then.

45

The young clergymen and gentlemen educated at the universities in the period of Laudian control had grown up, the first generation genuinely attached to 'High Church' values. They in turn gained control of the universities and passed on their views to another generation of ordinands and sons of gentlefolk. It was easy, moreover, to see a link between the collapse of the old Church in 1640 and the subsequent collapse of social discipline and of the traditional polity. Whatever the merits of Presbyterianism, it had failed to maintain discipline and subordination. It was hoped that restoring a hierarchical, authoritarian church would help to reinforce the traditional hierarchical and authoritarian social order which had seemed at times to be crumbling in the 1640s and 1650s. To many, the sects (especially the Quakers) stood for in-subordination — for setting the élite of the spirit against the traditional social élite, for challenging the age-old authority of squire and parson, for turning the world upside down. There were thus socio-political, as well as religious, reasons for restoring the old Church at the Restoration.

The rejection of comprehension and toleration in 1660–3 might have seemed decisive, but many refused to see it as final. Charles tried twice to allow some indulgence to Dissenters. Within the Church, there were many who disliked some features of the Restoration settlement. Hostile to the ritualism and rigidity of the High Churchmen, their consciences allowed them to subscribe to the new Prayer Book, but they sympathised with those who could not do so and tried to find ways of accommodating moderate Presbyterians within the Church. In the Exclusion Crisis the importance of the Dissenting vote and the High Churchmen's commitment to James's cause led the Whigs to take up the cause of toleration for Dissenters. A toleration bill narrowly failed to become law in 1681 and the failure of Exclusion, and the Tories' zest for revenge, brought a renewal of persecution in the early 1680s (**113**).

James's decision to abandon the Anglicans and appeal to the Dissenters reopened the question of toleration in an unexpected way. High Churchmen who had urged severity against Dissenters suddenly claimed to see the error of their ways. Most argued that James's offers of toleration were insincere, but many went further. In an effort to distract the Dissenters from James's blandishments, they called for Protestants to unite against the common enemy, Popery. Archbishop Sancroft and his bishops discussed possible reforms of the liturgy with leading Presbyterians, with a view to making the Church more comprehensive. They countered James's tolerationist propaganda by denying that the Church favoured persecution for conscience' sake, while Sancroft urged the parish clergy to greater diligence in looking after their flocks.

The Anglican leaders' attempts at a rapprochement with the Dissenters were in many ways successful, no doubt helped by Dissenters' suspicions of James's motives. In a gesture of solidarity which would have been inconceivable in 1685, a number of Dissenters visited the Seven Bishops in the Tower. Soon, however, the High Churchmen were to be as embarrassed by these overtures as the Tories were by their cautious welcome to William's invasion. It was one thing to build a common Protestant front against James. It was quite another to find oneself saddled with a foreign Calvinist king who favoured Dissenters, distrusted High Churchmen and gave a bishopric to Burnet, who was both a Whig and a Scot. Anxious Anglicans blamed William for the destruction of the episcopal church in Scotland, although it is doubtful whether he could have prevented it, and feared that the same would happen to the Church of England. By the beginning of 1689, the Church's leaders were having second thoughts about their promises to the Dissenters [**doc. 29**]. When it came to putting those promises into effect, they showed little enthusiasm.

The heads of grievances drawn up early in the Convention stated that laws should be passed 'for the liberty of Protestants in the exercise of their religion; and for uniting all Protestants in the matter of public worship, as far as may be' [**doc. 26**]. Thus comprehension and toleration were linked, as in 1660. A comprehension and a toleration bill were introduced in the Lords, where both received a second reading on 14 March 1689. Neither attracted much opposition until, on the 16th, William proposed the repeal of the Test and Corporation Acts, which excluded Dissenters from office, notably by requiring office-holders to take communion once a year in an Anglican Church. The proposal was rejected, but it had damaged the already meagre chances of the comprehension bill. The Presbyterians apart, none of the Dissenting denominations was interested in comprehension: their only concern was toleration. Even among the Presbyterians a new generation was emerging which saw no hope of reaching agreement with the Churchmen and was coming to accept sectarian status. Among the Anglicans, many had lost whatever zeal they had once felt for Protestant unity, now that the immediate need for it had passed. While the Lords discussed possible modifications to the service, more radical changes were proposed in a bill introduced in the Commons. A number of moderate Whigs, as well as the Tories, disliked this bill and by April both Houses had lost interest in comprehension, in effect leaving it to Convocation, which was to meet in the autumn. A committee of divines was set up to prepare proposals to set before Convocation, but it was plagued by disagreements [**doc. 30**] and Convocation rejected its proposals (**70, 113**).

Toleration attracted far less opposition than comprehension, but this did not mean that the principle of toleration was generally accepted. Most Dissenters did not care what happened to the Church's liturgy so long as they could worship as they pleased. Many of the Anglicans who fought to keep the Church's services unchanged were prepared, grudgingly, to admit that the Dissenters could never be bullied into conformity and perhaps even that they deserved some reward for resisting temptation under James. Thus while both Houses were prepared, in effect, to let comprehension die in Convocation, the toleration bill passed quite easily. The Toleration Act made no ringing statements about the virtues of tolerance, but stated prosaically that 'some ease to scrupulous consciences may be an effectual means to unite their majesties' Protestant subjects in interest and affection'. It repealed none of the laws against religious nonconformity, but exempted from the penalties of those laws all who were prepared to take the oath of allegiance and make the declaration against transubstantiation and other Catholic beliefs laid down in the 1678 Test Act. This allowed Protestant Dissenters (but not Catholics) to absent themselves from Church of England services and to worship freely, provided that the meeting place was notified to the civil or ecclesiastical authorities and that the doors were not locked. Dissenting clergymen could preach and minister freely, provided they took the same oath and declaration and subscribed to thirty-six of the Thirty-nine Articles. (Those which need not be taken related to homilies, to the consecration of bishops and ministers and to the authority of each national church to lay down what ceremonies it thought fit, even if these were not prescribed by the Bible.) Baptists could omit the reference to infant baptism in Article XXVII. The Act even took account of the Quakers' refusal to take oaths. They were allowed to declare (rather than swear) that they denied the pope's authority and that they believed in God the Father, and in Jesus Christ (**5**).

The Toleration Act was so drafted as to exclude from its benefits only Catholics, Socinians (who denied the divinity of Christ) and Jews. The Catholics apart (who could hardly hope for toleration so soon after James's reign) those excluded were very few indeed. In the range of denominations covered and the extent of religious liberty granted, the Toleration Act was without precedent, but Dissenters did not thereby become fully equal to Anglicans. The universities were still closed to them. They still had to pay tithes and church rates for the support of a church to which they did not belong. Above all, they were excluded from municipal and other offices by the need to take communion in order to qualify. While such disabilities remained, Dissenters were still second-class citizens. Their attempts to circumvent these restrictions were to cause great controversy in the generation after 1689.

The Toleration Act was not the final humiliation for the High Anglicans. One reason why the Tories in the Commons turned so strongly against comprehension was that the Whig majority insisted that the clergy should take the oath of allegiance to William and Mary. For many this was against their consciences, as it would involve breaking the oath of allegiance which they had sworn to James. Six bishops (including five of the seven who had petitioned James in 1688) and over four hundred of the lower clergy refused the oaths and were deprived of their benefices. Their departure was an unmitigated disaster for High Churchmen. Their decision to accept deprivation for conscience' sake was an implied reproach to other, more flexible, clergymen who took the oaths. It enabled the Whigs to denounce the High Church clergy – and the Tories in general – as more loyal to James than to William. Finally, it accelerated the replacement of the High Church bishops appointed by Charles and James with more moderate men. Thus the events of 1689 initiated a painful period of adjustment for the Church of England, and it is to the consequences of the Revolution settlement that we shall now turn.

Part Three: The Post-Revolution Order

Looking at the change of ruler, the Bill of Rights, the financial settlement and the Toleration Act, there seems little that was so dramatically new as to constitute a turning-point in English history, little that would merit the epithet 'Glorious' (or indeed, 'Revolution'). The significance of the change of ruler was limited and the Bill of Rights contained little that was new. Only the. Toleration Act marked a clear break with what had gone before. And yet the Revolution changed English government and politics profoundly and irrevocably — far more profoundly and irrevocably, indeed, than the great upheavals of 1640–60. One cause of this was undoubtedly the financial settlement. This was accompanied with no great statements of political philosophy. The failure to grant William an adequate independent revenue was quite deliberate, but it was a pragmatic, almost devious way of preventing him from abusing royal power, one which proved effective while raising no clear-cut issues of principle. Its effect was to be greatly accentuated by the French wars of 1689–97 and 1702–13. Both resulted directly from the Revolution. When William came to England, the Dutch were already at war with France. It was natural that James should seek refuge there and that Louis XIV should take up his cause. War against France thus became a matter of survival: if England did not fight, James would return with a French army. Similarly when James died in 1701, Louis impulsively recognised his son as James III, thus once again forcing England to join in a major continental war. These wars were on a scale England had never known before. They required larger armies and heavier taxes than England had ever experienced, which in turn imposed great strains on her administrative and political institutions. These strains were unexpected and unintended and the changes which they produced were complex. They were also often interrelated, which makes it artificial and misleading to treat them separately. With these points in mind, let us consider the salient features of the post-Revolution order.

7 The Growth of the Executive:
A Revolution in Government?

One obvious result of the wars was the expanded scale of government. The armed forces grew greatly in size, but so did the administrative departments which supplied and organised them and the revenue administration which raised the money to pay for them. The expansion perturbed and impressed contemporaries, even if the English administration was still small compared with that of (say) France. The ordnance office employed about sixty officers in 1683, 268 in 1692 and nearly 450 in 1704 (**114**). The expansion of the revenue administration had begun under Charles II. The change from revenue farming to direct collection led to the employment of hundreds of salaried officials throughout the country. By 1718 there were 561 full-time and around a thousand part-time customs officials in the port of London alone; even Great Yarmouth had 46 full-time and 56 part-time customs men. Excise officials were if anything more numerous. New duties like the salt and leather taxes required hundreds of officials to collect them — about five hundred in the case of the latter (**97**).

One result of the great increase in the scale of government and in the amount of money it handled was that incompetence and peculation appeared on a far larger scale. Henry Shales, who supplied victuals for the army in Ireland in 1689, was said to have paid nine pence for each pound of salt and sold it to the army for four shillings. His corruption and embezzlement were so systematic that one MP declared: 'If you want this war carried on with honour you must hang Shales' (**93**). Gentlemen who acted as land-tax officials were sometimes thousands of pounds in arrears. In the struggle between two rival East India companies in the 1690s, both sides resorted to large-scale bribery of politicians and civil servants. Each case of corruption that came to light convinced MPs and the general public that many others remained undiscovered.

Thus many suspected that much of the increased revenue from taxes passed illicitly into the pockets of civil servants and politicians, but the expansion of the executive seemed pernicious in another way. Wealth and authority were very unequally distributed in early modern society. The ruling élite of nobles and gentry was small but its members exercised great territorial influence through their wealth (as landlords, employers and consumers) and their rank, which enabled them to command respect and obedience in what was still a deferential society. These men saw themselves, and were seen by others, as the natural rulers of the shires. They dominated many parliamentary boroughs with small electorates and could influence substantial numbers of voters in the larger boroughs and the counties. Given their territorial influence,the crown had always had to enlist their co-operation if local government was to run smoothly. As Parliament became a more regular institution, their importance as MPs and as electoral patrons became greater still. In return for their co-operation and support, the crown had to offer 'patronage'. In the Tudor period this might consist of grants of land, leases of crown estates, marriage to a royal ward or economic concessions, such as monopolies. Under the later Stuarts two types of reward predominated — offices and pensions. With the expansion of the executive and the increased level of taxation, both became more abundant. Perhaps the greatest criticism of the expansion of the executive was that it created more jobs to be used as political patronage. Anxiety was expressed about the growing number of officials and military men in the Commons: indeed, a few categories were declared ineligible for membership. At a local level, the multiplication of revenue officials threatened to make them a significant, perhaps even a decisive, element in the electorates of many small boroughs. Perhaps the greatest argument against Walpole's excise scheme of 1733 was that it would require so many new officials that they would, in effect, take over the electoral system (**83**). The fears that were so widely expressed about the growth of the crown's patronage resources were not groundless. Ambitious politicians naturally hoped to use the places at their disposal to build a following. As party rivalry intensified, offices in the administration, the armed forces and the Church became the objects of party competition. Party leaders pressed the monarch to give their followers a monopoly of office. However, a full-scale 'spoils system' (whereby offices were filled purely on political criteria) did not develop. Neither William nor Anne wished either party to have a monopoly of office, for that would make the monarch a virtual prisoner of the party leaders. Moreover, many administrators resisted the pressure to turn their offices into political pawns. The seventeenth century saw important changes in the nature of office-holding. At the beginning, offices were seen as a form of property. Men were appointed to offices because their patrons were in favour at court or because their fathers had held them. Salaries were usually minimal and officials made most of their income from fees, gratuities and other less legitimate perquisites. Most officials bitterly resisted administrative reform, because reform might reduce the volume of business they handled and therefore their profits.

Even before the Revolution there were signs of change. Reliance on fees and gratuities (not to say bribes) had not disappeared, as Pepys's diary makes clear. Army commissions were bought and sold; colonels received a lump sum for their regiments, which encouraged them to falsify their muster rolls and cheat the soldiers. However, more and more officials were paid adequate salaries and were no longer dependent on fees. This was true especially among subordinate officials and those in the rapidly expanding revenue administration: yet again, the switch to direct collection of the customs and excise marks a turning-point. Along with an increasing regularity in the methods of payment went an increasing regularity of bureaucratic routine: Pepys, with his obsession for neatness, order and method can be seen as a harbinger of a new era. This was the time when administrators first used statistics systematically, when the treasury commission of 1667 tried to impose some system on the chaos of royal spending, when Charles Davenant tried to bully officials in the newly-established excise administration into following regular routines. It was impossible to change overnight a system that was, in many ways, still that of the Middle Ages. The Exchequer continued to issue notched willow twigs (tallies) as receipts until the nineteenth century — but even these tallies were increasingly used as instruments of short-term borrowing (**43**). Sinecures persisted, especially in the older departments. In the newer departments, formal routine and non-political appointments were most apparent at the subordinate level: at the top, informal methods and political appointments remained common (**114**). Even so, the growing professionalism of the expanding civil service helped it to cope with tasks different qualitatively and quantitatively from those of the past. It was also able, for a while, to resist with some success the politicians' attempts to use all offices for party political advantage. After 1714 the Whigs gained a monopoly of offices at every level, but not all the benefits of the new professionalism were lost. The Whig ascendancy brought stability of personnel and not all those appointed as a result of party favour were incompetent hacks. Routines and methods established under the later Stuarts had acquired the force of habit. Even so, after 1714 the pace of change slackened markedly. Not until the mid-nineteenth century did the civil service undergo another transformation in terms of size, organisation and attitudes as profound as that of the later Stuart period.

8 The Financial Revolution

If the later seventeenth century saw the emergence of an increasingly professional civil service, it also saw the development of a far more rational and efficient system of taxation. Before 1641, the crown relied mainly on its patrimonial and feudal revenues, derived from its lands, its feudal rights and various aspects of its prerogative (impositions, monopolies and ship money, for example). Of the permanent, 'ordinary' revenues only the customs (granted for life to most monarchs) could strictly be described as taxation. There was no regular form of taxation on the main source of wealth, land. The subsidies which Parliament voted were irregular and unproductive, not least because the more influential landowners made sure that their wealth was grossly underassessed. The crown was thus ill-equipped to tap its subjects' wealth. Inability to tax that wealth effectively drove successive monarchs to use archaic, dubiously legal and often very inefficient methods of raising money, which usually provoked political resentment. By 1641 that resentment had become so overwhelming that Charles I was forced to abandon many of his sources of income. When, after the enforced hiatus of the civil wars, the Parliaments of the early 1660s considered the royal revenue, they had to make what was, in effect, a fresh start, calculating how much the king would need and voting revenues intended to yield that amount. They were also able to insist that Charles II should raise money only in ways approved by Parliament. He was granted the customs, as in the past, but also received the excise (levied mainly on alcoholic drinks consumed within England, first imposed during the civil wars) and the hearth money, a crude property tax. The experience gained in the civil wars was seen also in the use of the monthly assessment for extraordinary taxation, rather than the old subsidy. Whereas in the subsidy taxpayers gave in an estimate, often highly fanciful, of their net income from land, in the assessment each county had to meet a quota, which was apportioned between the taxpayers roughly in proportion to their wealth. By such means, more money was raised than under the subsidy and the burden was distributed more equitably (**32**).

After 1660, the crown's methods of raising money were more rational and efficient than before. It could levy permanent taxes on overseas trade and some areas of consumption at home and, if need arose, Parliament would vote reasonably equitable temporary taxes on landed income. These taxes were fiscally more efficient than the crown's old feudal and prerogative revenues. They were also far less contentious and unpopular, for they had been voted by Parliament and did not depend on dubious interpretations of the law. As it turned out, the revenues granted to Charles II yielded so much that by the 1680s he no longer needed to call Parliament. William's parliaments had no intention of making such a mistake again. As we have seen, they were careful not to give him sufficient to 'live of his own', but the basic trend towards a more rational and efficient taxation of the nation's wealth continued. There were some new customs duties and many new excises. Taxation on land, traditionally imposed only in emergencies, became so frequent as to be permanent and the level of the land tax increased. Although the unpopular monthly assessment, using county quotas, was abandoned and there was a return to individual assessment, this was much more accurate than in the past. It tended to become fixed and it could be predicted that a land tax of a shilling in the pound would yield about half a million pounds, so in practice it differed little from the monthly assessment, in that its yield was substantial and predictable. The Revolution also accelerated a process which had begun in the civil wars and continued under Charles II, whereby the English became used to paying taxes. In France this was achieved largely by using soldiers to break the taxpayers' resistance, but this was not the case in England (at least after 1660). The fact that all taxation was by Parliament's consent undoubtedly helped, but so did the fact that it became regular and predictable, a matter of routine. In the case of the land tax, the fact that local bigwigs were responsible for supervising its assessment and collection made the increased amount and the increased frequency more bearable (**27**). In the case of the excise, which was often violently unpopular in the Interregnum and even under Charles II, the tax was collected by a hierarchy of professional officials, controlled from London, and not by local volunteers. Yet even this system, alien though it was to traditional patterns of local self-government, became accepted in time. Men became accustomed to the routine of search and inspection. By Anne's reign it was not uncommon for brewers to leave the key so that the excisemen could inspect the brewing if they were out.

All this made it possible for William III to levy far more in taxation than Charles I or Elizabeth could have dreamed of. Charles I's average annual revenue was under one million pounds. James II's was around two million. William III's, in peace and war, was about four and a half million, with the land tax alone bringing in as much as two million. This massive increase in yield was achieved with his subjects' consent, a consent expressed not only through Parliament but also through those who administered the land tax at a local level. William III was more dependent on parliament for money than any of his predecessors, but he was able to levy far more in taxation and to fight wars on a far larger scale than ever before. Co-operation with parliament, enforced though it might be, proved much more lucrative than financial independence. This co-operation, moreover, was not confined to taxation. It could also be seen in the sphere of government borrowing and here, more than in the case of taxation, the Revolution marked the start of a new era.

The inadequacy of the crown's ordinary revenue, and the slowness with which money came in, had long forced kings to borrow to meet immediate needs. All the Stuarts were permanently in debt, but until Charles II's reign crown borrowing was haphazard and unsystematic. The king might levy forced loans, or fail to pay tradesmen's bills, or negotiate short-term loans with whoever could be persuaded to take the risk. Lenders could not be sure that they would be repaid in full (or at all): much depended on whether they had powerful friends at court. Tradesmen charged inflated prices, to allow for the probable delay or default in the payment of their bills. Such a lack of system and predictability made borrowing difficult and expensive. Charles II's reign saw the first signs of a more rational system. In 1665 the Act for the Additional Aid of £1,250,000 (towards the Dutch War) laid down a procedure whereby the Exchequer could borrow (either directly or by delaying payments to government creditors) at 6 per cent. The orders authorising payment were to be numbered and paid in strict chronological order. For the first time, repayment became a matter of routine, not of personal favour, and the small investor could lend to the crown and be confident of being repaid. Much of the benefit of this arrangement was lost when the Stop of the Exchequer of 1672 suspended the repayment of capital (although not the payment of interest) on the Exchequer's debts, and in the 1680s interest payments also fell seriously into arrears. Thus on the eve of the Revolution, the crown's credit with both large and small investors was considerably shaken (**43, 105**).

With the French war and the inadequate provision for William's ordinary revenue, borrowing was a necessity. The level of government indebtedness increased greatly, but there was no attempt like that of 1665 to reorganise government borrowing: improvisation and muddling through were the order of the day. Parliament soon accepted that the war was too expensive to be paid for out of current income and began to vote certain taxes, not to be spent directly on the war, but to pay interest on loans from the public or on debts already incurred. As few expected the war of 1689−97 to last as long as it did, the Commons concentrated on short-term rather than long-term borrowing. They also consistently overestimated the yields of the taxes they voted to service this borrowing, which made it hard to pay interest promptly and in full. However, the very fact that Parliament now met annually and seemed a more permanent and regular institution strengthened the credit of a system which depended substantially on anticipating the yield of future taxes. With Parliament's position secure, those taxes were more likely to be voted and collected. From 1692, the Commons listened more attentively to schemes for long-term borrowing. The interest on the 'tontine' loan of 1693 (in which surviving investors received more and more as others died off) was provided by excise duties voted for ninety-nine years. More important was the Tonnage Act of 1694. This provided for a loan of £1,200,000 at 8 per cent and for the subscribers to be incorporated as the Bank of England, empowered to deal in bills of exchange. The Bank was to prove invaluable as a means of attracting deposits from small investors which could then be lent to the government, but this system could not have worked without the confidence which stemmed from the Bank's resting on an Act of Parliament.

The tontine and the Bank were early signs of a system of government credit resting on long-term borrowing, underpinned by Act of Parliament, rather than short-term borrowing through the anticipation of taxes and the delayed payment of government creditors. Under William, such long-term loans accounted for much less than half of the sixteen and a half million pounds borrowed during the French wars. The reliance on short-term expedients meant that the rate of interest was high − on average 8.3 per cent, at a time of stable prices. It was nevertheless a considerable achievement to borrow an average of some two million pounds a year (more than Charles II's average annual revenue) at a time when taxes were at an unprecedented level and the economy was disrupted by war and by a complete overhaul of the coinage.

Without this borrowing, which accounted for one third of all expenditure in 1689—97, the war could not have been carried on. Mistakes were made, but the reign marked the start of a new era in British government finance, when war was paid for by borrowing as well as by taxation. Given the spiralling cost of warfare, this was the only way in which a comparatively small country like Britain could afford to fight larger countries like France. Gradually, it came to be accepted that the debts incurred in wartime were too large to be fully repaid when peace returned. The national debt, from being an embarrassment, came to be seen as a permanent institution and a secure investment. Resting as they did on the credit of the nation, not the word of a king, British government securities attracted investors from the continent as well as Britain. As it became easier to attract lenders, the rate of interest fell. Under Anne, Godolphin placed more emphasis on long-term annuities and less on short-term anticipations and used the Bank and the East India Company to attract larger loans from the public. Growing confidence in the government's credit, encouraged by military success, enabled him to increase the level of borrowing to an average of over two and a half million a year, while cutting interest rates to below 7 per cent. After the peace of 1713 interest rates fell steadily to reach 3 per cent or less by the 1730s. A sense of pride in this achievement was captured in a pamphlet of 1733 (**43**):

> There can't be a stronger proof of that high esteem which the people of England, and the neighbouring nations also, entertain for our glorious constitution than the immense credit our legislature has found in borrowing of money. It is not probable that the greatest absolute monarch could, in his most extensive dominions, raise by voluntary contributions a loan of fifty millions of money. And yet France, Turkey, Persia, India and China severally yield much larger annual revenues than Great Britain.

The Glorious Revolution marked a turning-point in the government's ability to raise money and to wage war, which reflected an increase in both the revenue from taxation and government borrowing. The war of 1689—97 cost about five and a half million pounds a year, that of 1702—13 about eight and a half million, that of 1756—63 about twenty-three million. In each case about one-third of the cost was met by borrowing and two-thirds from taxation (**43**). This had two major consequences. First, Britain became a major European and world power. Henry VIII's reign had shown that Tudor England was a second-class power. In the

1520s his mounting demands for taxation provoked a taxpayers' strike. In the 1540s, wary of provoking the taxpayers again, he financed his wars by selling off vast tracts of monastic land (thus wasting the Tudor crown's only opportunity to achieve an adequate financial foundation) and by ruinous debasements of the coinage. Elizabeth defeated the Spanish armadas with the help of a large measure of luck and took nine years to suppress a rebellion in Ireland. The Cadiz fiasco and the Medway disaster showed that Charles I and Charles II lacked the financial resources to fight a major war. Only Cromwell, who had an experienced army and could raise taxes by force, could afford a positive foreign policy. After 1689, the contrast was enormous. Anne's armies ranged from the Netherlands to Bavaria and Spain. England became the prime mover of the great coalition against France. This dramatic change in England's European role was made possible only by the dramatic improvement in the government's ability to raise money, which in turn was made possible only by the crown's ability to win the nation's co-operation, through Parliament and great financial institutions like the East India Company and the Bank.

The second major consequence of the 'financial revolution' stemmed from the growth of these financial institutions. The fact that they could mobilise such vast sums gave them a potentially huge political influence. It was widely feared that they might hold the government to ransom by cutting off the flow of loans. The Bank's directors tried to exert such pressure in 1710, in an effort to prevent Godolphin's dismissal, but they failed and Harley built up the South Sea Company as an alternative source of loans. In fact, fears of the great corporations' malign political influence proved largely unfounded. There was more substance to more general complaints of the rise of the 'monied interest'. The vast increase in government borrowing meant that bankers and financiers prospered as never before. Some became enormously and ostentatiously rich and bought their way into Parliament. In the past, most successful financiers had also been involved in trade and, having made their fortunes, they had bought country estates and sought to merge into the gentry. Many of the new monied men were not actively involved in trade (a less attractive proposition than usual, because of the ravages of war), nor did they leave the City to add new blood and new wealth to the landed élite. Land was taxed more heavily than ever before, agricultural prices were sluggish and rents were low, so there was little economic incentive for *nouveaux riches* to buy land. Many landowners found it hard to find satisfactory tenants and had to write off rent arrears in bad years. They thus found it particularly galling that men of humble or even immigrant origins (Huguenots or Netherlanders) were becoming so rich that they could sometimes outbid country gentlemen for the support of the electorate, while landowners struggled to maintain their standard of living. Many claimed that the wars were part of a great conspiracy whereby money was transferred, via the land tax and government borrowing, from the pockets of the landowners to those of the monied men [**doc. 31**].

Before 1688 England's society and government were dominated by landowners, their temporary eclipse in the 1640s and 1650s making them doubly determined to reassert what they saw as their rightful primacy. One key to the landed élite's continued dominance was its willingness to absorb new wealth acquired elsewhere: the parvenus of one century became the established county families of the next. What was so obnoxious about the new monied men was partly the extent of their wealth, partly their unwillingness to be absorbed, to recognise that social status could not be attained without land. For a while it seemed that the landowners' dominance over government and society was in jeopardy and this sense of threat explains the bitter attacks on the monied men in Anne's reign. The return of peace meant a cut in the land tax and a halt to government borrowing, while the circle of those investing in government funds widened to include many landowners. The animosities of Anne's reign died down, the great financial institutions came to be accepted as part of the natural order of things. By the mid-eighteenth century the monied men had been quietly absorbed into a ruling class that was once more united and self-confident (**108**). This process of absorption can be seen in the case of Samson Gideon, who enjoyed great influence in government circles in the 1750s, despite being not only a financier but also a Jew. His son became a Christian and an Irish peer.

9 Religion After the Revolution

The Church of England

The Toleration Act recognised, somewhat belatedly, the existence of the religious pluralism which had been a fact of life since the 1640s. No longer would the state assist the ecclesiastical authorities in their efforts to punish those who did not wish to attend Anglican services. Yet if dissent from the established church was now legally permissible, the Church none the less remained established. The year 1689 saw the start of a somewhat illogical process whereby the Church gradually lost the practical benefits of establishment, though never losing an established status which proved a mixed blessing. While other denominations could adapt their organisation or liturgy at will, the Church of England could do so only with Parliament's approval: to create a new parish required an Act of Parliament. Moreover, the benefits which the Church retained in 1689 turned out to be more apparent than real. As the Toleration Act made no provision for checking on the orthodoxy of schoolteachers, the Church lost its monopoly of education, except at university level. Even there its advantages were eroded in practice, as the two English universities subsided into a complacent intellectual torpor while the Dissenting academies became renowned for their academic vigour. Perhaps the Church's greatest advantage after 1689 was the Anglican monopoly of public office and of political power, but this monopoly was undermined by the practice of occasional conformity: many Dissenters took communion in an Anglican church once a year in order to qualify for office.

For Churchmen who had insisted so loudly and so successfully on uniformity in the 1660s and early 1680s, the loss of the Church's position of supremacy came as a profound shock. Worse was to follow. The lapsing of the Licensing Act in 1695 destroyed the last vestige of clerical control over the press: no longer would works of theology require the approval of a leading churchman. The end of censorship was followed by a small flurry of publications which advocated deism or even atheism. To many, these publications were symptomatic of a collapse of traditional spiritual and moral values, seen also in the Toleration Act, the deprivation of the non-jurors, occasional conformity, rampant corruption in public life and the lewdness of many stage plays. The 1690s seemed a time of brash innovation, full of projects of financial change, when fortunes were made overnight by dubious means and when the old order and values of rural society were under attack. Nothing was taken for granted or immune from questioning. Such an atmosphere — amoral, experimental and above all metropolitan — was profoundly alien to traditional Anglicans. Their values were those of village society, stable and unchanging, where the squire-magistrate and parson enforced traditional Christian morality and drove recalcitrant peasants to church. Village life was dominated by deference on one hand and paternalism on the other: behind both lay a strong sense of ancient and immutable hierarchy.

The contrast between London and the country, between (on one hand) the brash, hectic, cynical world of government, business and finance and (on the other) the unchanging routines of agriculture, had always existed but had never seemed so stark as in the 1690s. As Dissenters went into open competition with the Church and circumvented the law to break in upon the Anglicans' monopoly of office, as jumped-up immigrant bankers made huge fortunes while agriculture languished, as atheism and immorality seemed to flourish unchecked, the Churchmen's resentment grew into a deep, bitter anger. They might have little influence in the big corporations, but they had numbers on their side and they controlled the majority of pulpits in the villages and small towns where most English people lived. They had the great asset of speaking for tradition in a conservative society and of an ideal of the social order whose roots lay deep in the past, an ideal which still bore some resemblance to reality and which appeared all the more perfect in comparison with an unappealing present (**24, 49**) [**doc. 33**].

The Churchmen's discomfiture under William was compounded by their own divisions. The High Church element was the largest. Since 1660 the universities had turned out hundreds of High Church parsons and imbued the sons of the gentry with High Church principles. Like Laud they held that visual richness and the eucharist were as important as preaching and were attached to the Prayer Book service in its entirety. They believed episcopacy to be the only divinely ordained form of church government, so had little sympathy for Dissenters or foreign non-episcopal churches. The High Church clergy and laity had provided much of the impetus and ideology of the Tory reaction of the 1680s. Angered and perplexed by James's conduct, most High Churchmen clung to their principles of legitimism and non-resistance and took the oaths to the new rulers reluctantly, if at all. Some claimed that they had taken them only in order to carry on the fight against those they saw as the Church's enemies — the Low Churchmen and Latitudinarians.

These two elements within the Church were often lumped together, but should be distinguished. The Low Church proper represented a continuation of the moderate Puritan tradition of the reigns of Elizabeth and James I, which had found a somewhat uncomfortable home among the Presbyterians of the 1640s and 1650s. Its spirit was expressed by clergymen like Ralph Josselin (who conformed under Charles II, but almost never wore a surplice) and Richard Baxter, who refused to conform in 1662, but never regarded himself as a Dissenter and had far more in common with most Low Churchmen than with doctrinaire Presbyterians. Low Churchmen wanted a simple service, uncluttered by ceremonies, and with the main stress placed on preaching the Word: they stood firmly in the evangelical tradition of English Puritanism [**doc. 32**].

The Latitudinarians, by contrast, were products of a newer intellectual climate. Low Churchmen, like most Puritans, maintained the traditional Christian emphasis on human frailty and depravity. Man fought a constant losing battle against his own sinful nature and could not begin to understand God's complex and inscrutable purposes. All he could do was cling to God's word by basing his actions on the literal interpretation of the Bible. The Latitudinarians' outlook, however, reflected both an increased confidence in human potential and weariness with wranglings about the precise meaning of the more obscure passages of the Bible. Advances in scientific understanding made some wonder if man really was such an insignificant blemish on the face of creation. Copernicus and Galileo, Newton and Harvey, showed that the universe and even the human body seemed to function according to ascertainable mathematical laws. Phenomena which had once seemed the capricious actions of a severe and vengeful God were now explained, and the belief grew that others, still inexplicable, would one day be understood. God receded from the foreground of everyday life to the background: instead of intervening constantly in earthly affairs, he had set in motion a marvellously complex set of mechanisms which now functioned independently.

The Latitudinarians argued that one should not pore over the textual minutiae of the Bible but seek to deduce the broad underlying themes, the basic moral precepts which underlay the elaborate rules of conduct of the Old Testament. To them, God no longer appeared an interminably demanding tyrant, insisting that men justify every action. He now seemed the benevolent architect of a delightfully rational universe, in which man wandered at will, using his own judgement. The emphasis in moral theology changed, from an obsession with sin and human inadequacy (the hallmark of Puritanism) to a simple, undemanding prudential morality. To live a good life was easy, pleasant and profitable. Such an outlook suited those weary of the excesses of Puritan zeal and those who had faith in human reason and human dignity. It had no place for the torments of hell, for the agony of doubt or, indeed, for strong emotions of any kind. So concerned were the Latitudinarians to avoid 'enthusiasm' that they made religion bland and undemanding to the point of dullness [**doc. 34**]. Some were so concerned to avoid dogmatism that they reduced the essentials of belief almost to nothing. Locke (a man of piety, in his own way) claimed that the only belief essential to salvation was that Jesus was the Messiah. Similar views could be found among the clergy. Samuel Clarke (despite subscribing to the Thirty-Nine Articles) did not believe in the Trinity. The High Churchmen's *bête noire*, Benjamin Hoadly, went futher. He claimed that God required only that one should be sincere in one's beliefs: He had laid down no dogmas or doctrines. Any church was as good as any other — indeed, there was no need for churches at all (which would remove any pretext for persecution). For High Churchmen, who believed that the Church of England derived its authority from Scripture and from its antiquity, and that its government and rituals were divinely ordained, it was intolerable that a man with such beliefs should be an Anglican priest. Hoadly, however, not only remained within the Church but prospered mightily, thanks to the patronage of Whig politicians, who relished Hoadly's quasi-Lockean political pamphlets almost as much as his outspoken attacks on High Churchmen. Despite his denial of the need for churches, Hoadly sought preferment eagerly and ended his days in the plum bishopric of Winchester in the reign of George II (**110**).

The opposition to High Churchmen within the Church of England thus consisted partly of old-style Puritans and partly of new-style Latitudinarians. By the early eighteenth century the latter were far more influential than the former and were becoming known, rather confusingly, as Low Churchmen. They agreed with traditional Puritans in placing little emphasis on ceremonies and in a tolerant attitude towards Dissenters. On ceremonies, the High Churchmen to some extent got their way. Before the civil wars, church interiors had been plain and whitewashed, with a communion table in the body of the church. Laud's orders to move the table to the east end of the church, placed altarwise and railed off from the people, had been treated as a detestable Popish innovation. By the end of the century, however, Laud's views had triumphed, in so far as most churches had altars and the bareness of their interiors was mitigated by a few ornaments and improving texts. Most of the clergy wore the surplice which the Puritans had so detested (**117**). On other matters, the High Churchmen fought a losing battle. They had the advantage of numbers, but most bishoprics under William and Anne went to Low Churchmen, Latitudinarians or moderates. William's sympathies were Calvinist and he and Mary resented the High Churchmen's reluctance to recognise them as 'rightful and lawful' monarchs. Anne was a good Anglican, but turned against the High Churchmen after they threatened, in 1704, to hold up the money needed for the war in order to force through a bill against occasional conformity. Only one rabid High Churchman, Atterbury, became a bishop between 1689 and 1714. The rest were mostly, in Burnet's phrase, 'men both of moderate principles and of calm tempers' (**2, 25**). Thus if the Church was to speak with their voice, the High Church clergy had first to impose their wishes on the bishops and this led to the demand for the recall of Convocation [**doc. 33**]. Meanwhile, their impotence within the Church led them to rely on the help of their lay allies in Parliament. With their strong sense of the need to maintain the traditional close connection between church and state, it seemed natural to use political means to achieve ecclesiastical ends.

Convocation was the clerical equivalent of Parliament. The Upper House consisted of the bishops, the Lower of representatives of the lesser clergy. In 1689 the Lower House proved so truculent and intractable over the comprehension proposals that William decided that it should never meet again, but in the later 1690s High Churchmen pressed insistently for its recall. Lay politicians whose support William needed in order to manage Parliament (notably Rochester) insisted that it should meet, as a condition of their accepting office. From 1701 to 1717 it met each year, in parallel with Parliament. Each year the bishops used various methods to delay proceedings in the Lower House. Although some useful ecclesiastical business was conducted — that, after all, was Convocation's ostensible purpose — the High Churchmen's attempts to use Convocation as a political weapon were largely unsuccessful (**24, 67**)

If the High Churchmen failed to win control of Convocation, they were more successful in elections and in the Commons, where force of numbers counted for more. Under Anne, religion once again became a major political issue. In the last years of her reign, an overwhelmingly Tory Commons secured the passing of Acts against occasional conformity and Dissenting schools, but these successes were short-lived. When the Whigs regained power in 1714, these Acts were soon repealed. Convocation ceased to meet. The Tories became an impotent minority in the Commons. All the top posts in the Church went to Whigs, including the obnoxious Hoadly. High Church views now had no means of expression. Ambitious young clerics soon saw that there was no future in High Churchmanship. (Bishop Gibson of London, who was both a High Churchman and a Whig, was perhaps the exception that proves the rule.) High Church values survived, at Oxford and in many parishes, but had no influence in the upper reaches of the Church. Latitudinarianism had triumphed. The Church advanced into the eighteenth century, eschewing enthusiasm, its top posts the objects of political patronage. While many Anglican priests and laymen showed sincere, if undemonstrative, piety, this was a Church without strong emotions, run by the laity for the benefit of the laity (**110**).

Dissent

Predictably, the Church was adversely affected by the Toleration Act. Attendance at its services fell sharply, as not only Dissenters but also the apathetic and indifferent could now stay away with impunity. Where there was a resident squire to put pressure on the parishioners, attendances remained high. Without such pressures, and in more scattered communities, the Church lost most of its adherents, but this does not mean that Dissent prospered. The number of Dissenters probably increased in the quarter century after 1689, to reach maybe half a million in 1715 (out of a population of nearly six million). This increase was helped by immigration, notably of thousands of Calvinists from the Palatinate. However, the geographical incidence of Dissent was uneven. Its main strength lay in the larger, more industrial towns. In rural areas of the South and Midlands it was weak, but in the North and Wales the age-old deficiencies of the established church had left a religious vacuum which had been partly filled (in different places) by Baptists,

Quakers and even Catholics. The brief flurry of expansion after 1689 was soon over. By the 1720s and 1730s all denominations were suffering a serious decline in numbers (**54, 67**).

One could ascribe this decline to a cooling of fervour once the pressure of persecution was removed, but it would probably have occurred even without the Toleration Act. Evangelical movements have always shown a tendency to run out of steam. It is hard to sustain the commitment which stems from the initial excitement of conversion. As numbers grow, emphasis shifts from expansion to consolidation. Wealthy adherents wish to invest their money and effort in fine chapels rather than new missionary efforts. There are disputes about doctrine or organisation, within or between denominations. There are fewer new recruits, while old adherents (and, still more, their children) fall away. Such processes could be seen in English Dissent in the early eighteenth century. The Presbyterians, after the failure of comprehension (yet again) in 1689, became resigned to sectarian status. They were also increasingly infected by the rationalism which spawned the Latitudinarians within the Church of England. More and more moved away from their Calvinist roots towards heterodoxy, especially on the Trinity. They lost many of their less educated, more traditionally minded adherents and became the most intellectual of Dissenting denominations. Indeed, they eventually lost all connection with old-style presbyterianism and became Unitarians (**26**). While the Presbyterians abandoned their Puritan roots, others clung to them more closely. Congregationalists and Baptists became increasingly inward-looking and rigid, abandoning the evangelism and doctrinal flexibility of their formative years for an obsession with doctrinal purity. The Quakers shed their initial eccentricities and exhibitionism and subsided into a quietist respectability whose chief effect was a continual dwindling of numbers (**54**). Thus while Latitudinarianism dominated the Church of England, Old Dissent subsided into blandness or introspection. The fire of the Puritanism of the first half of the seventeenth century seemed dead. It was revived by the Methodists, who rediscovered that (in John Wesley's words) faith was 'not barely a speculative, rational thing, a cold lifeless assent, a train of ideas in the head; but also a disposition of the heart... . It is a sure confidence which a man hath in God that, through the merits of Christ, *his* sins are forgiven and *he* reconciled to the favour of God' (**25**).

To many in the mid-eighteenth century, Methodism seemed a throwback to an earlier age. Wesley was unusual among educated men in seeing everything in the Bible as the Word of God (and in believing in witches). The Toleration Act may have been the product of the circumstances of 1689, not of a formed belief in toleration, but by the mid-eighteenth century most people had come to see religion as a private matter and no concern of the state. The Latitudinarian emphasis on the basic essentials of Christianity and on the common ground between Protestant denominations had triumphed over the dogmatic, intolerant certainties of High Churchman and Puritan alike. Even the Catholics, long regarded as a political threat, came to seem less dangerous after the failure of the Jacobite rebellion of 1745. In practice, they could worship as they wished and 1791 saw the first tentative step towards Catholic emancipation. It would be naive to see the Toleration Act as the sole reason for this new tolerance. Clearly it was a product of intellectual developments which dated back to the mid-seventeenth century and which were by no means confined to England (**62**). Nevertheless, the fact that the Act *had* been passed strengthened the position of the advocates of toleration. Despite the High Churchmen's dire warnings, experience was to show that religious toleration did not inevitably lead to anarchy. The reasons for passing the Act were practical rather than ideological, yet belief in the principle of toleration, which had existed well before 1689, was greatly strengthened by the simple fact that toleration now existed and could be seen to work. Once again pragmatism emerges as the salient feature of the Glorious Revolution.

10   The Constitution: Crown and Parliament

As we have already seen, the Declaration of Rights was a limited and conservative document. Its main concern was to prevent a recurrence of the misgovernment of Charles II and James II. Only in a negative sense did it define the future relationship of crown and Parliament. The more novel proposals contained in the programme of possible legislation were dropped before the Declaration was read to William and Mary. The evolution of the post-Revolution constitution owed far less to the Bill of Rights than to the crown's new financial weakness and to the unprecedented administrative, financial and political strains created by the French wars. As a result of these new conditions, the relationship of crown and Parliament developed in a way that few could have predicted in 1689. Parliament now met each year, for several months: it became, in effect, a permanent institution. The royal prerogative, for so long a potential threat to liberty and property, was now effectively curbed. Meanwhile, the growth of the executive and of the crown's financial resources created the possibility that the crown might be able to control Parliament by means of places and pensions [**doc. 36**]. The 'influence' of the crown thus came to seem a greater threat than the prerogative to the integrity of Parliament and the well-being of those it represented. This threat was never entirely realised, but under George I and II skilful use of the crown's patronage was a major factor in its successful management of Parliament.

The crown's continued success in managing Parliament, however, obscures a change of fundamental importance. By George II's reign the king's personal role in government was much smaller than in the seventeenth century. It was now the king's ministers who controlled the administration, managed Parliament and exploited the crown's patronage, and although they owed their places in part to the king's favour, the king's choice was limited to men who could manage the Commons. Thus the relationship of king and Commons had changed more than was at first apparent, but the most profound change lay in the relationship between king and ministers, between the king and the politicians.

The post-Revolution period saw some new statutory restrictions on the crown, which mostly reflected the new conditions of William's reign rather than the implementation of the programme of 1689. The king's freedom to call and dismiss Parliament was curtailed by the Triennial Act of 1694, which reflected fears of the 'influence of the crown'. The earlier Triennial Acts of 1641 and 1664 had been concerned to ensure that Parliament met at least once every three years. Now that Parliament met annually, concern shifted to the danger that a long-standing Parliament might be corrupted by means of places and pensions. Under the 1694 Act there was to be a general election at least once every three years: in fact, there were ten in the next twenty years and the country remained almost continually in the grip of election fever. This Act was repealed by the Septennial Act of 1716, under which a Parliament could remain in being for seven years. The other major piece of restrictive legislation was the Act of Settlement of 1701. This vested the succession (after Anne) in the House of Hanover, but the mainly Tory House of Commons showed its dislike of William and of the prospect of another foreign king by laying down various restrictions which were to come into force when Anne died. These showed a mixture of xenophobia (as with the prohibition on foreigners' holding office) and suspicion of the influence of the crown (as with the exclusion of *all* office-holders from Parliament) [**doc. 35**].

Of the legislative proposals in the 'heads of grievances' of 1689, few reached the statute book. The prohibition of the monarch's marrying a Catholic was included in the Bill of Rights. Acts were passed in 1689 for toleration (but not comprehension) and a new coronation oath. Of the rest, the Triennial Act prevented the 'too long continuance' of any Parliament; an Act of 1696 regulated treason trials; and the judges' tenure was changed by the Act of Settlement, so that they could no longer be dismissed without Parliament's consent. (This harked back to James II's purges of the judiciary: William had not put pressure on his judges in this way.) The Act of Settlement also declared that a royal pardon could not save a person from impeachment, an item included in the first draft of the 'heads of grievances' but not the final version. It was incorporated in the Act of Settlement because the Tories hoped to impeach the Whig ministers who until recently had dominated William's administration. For the rest, the demands for the abolition of the hearth tax and for frequent sessions of Parliament were rendered irrelevant by events: William voluntarily gave up the hearth money and it soon became clear that Parliament would now meet each year. Attempts to stamp out electoral corruption and to reform the legal system bore little fruit. The Elections Act of 1696 said nothing of bribery or treating and concentrated mainly on sheriffs' malpractices. With William showing no inclination to pervert the electoral and legal systems, the twin forces of inertia and vested interest were sufficient to prevent change. Besides, these old issues seemed less pressing as new and more urgent problems arose. (**52, 69**).

The restrictions imposed by statute on the prerogative were thus limited. The king still had the power to call and dismiss Parliament at will (subject to the Triennial, and later the Septennial, Act), to choose his ministers, to direct the administration and to formulate policy. Most of these powers still belong to the crown in theory, but in practice monarchs have found it more and more difficult to exercise them. One of the peculiarities of the British constitution is the great difference between the crown's theoretical and actual powers. This difference was the product of financial and political pressures which developed from 1689. These imposed limitations on the crown (some embodied in 'conventions', some not) far more constricting than those imposed by statute (**76**). The crucial factor was the crown's financial dependence on Parliament. MPs had long talked of 'redress before supply', the need for grievances to be redressed before money was granted. Before 1640 the crown had had far too many independent sources of revenue for such demands to be effective. Even under Charles II, the king's financial position was seldom so desperate that he had to succumb to such pressures (**87**). After 1689, however, when MPs invoked the principle of 'redress before supply', they knew they possessed the financial power to get their way. William knew it too. He avoided measures which might antagonise the Commons, while politicians sometimes used the threat of blocking supply in an effort to intimidate him. In 1690 Halifax noted that William 'said he would not have the bill of corporations pass. Said that some of the party that pressed it had sent him word that if he interposed or meddled in it, they would not finish the money bills' (**9**). More blatant was the practice of 'tacking' clauses on other matters to money bills. By tradition, the Lords could not amend money bills, so the Lords and king had to choose between passing such bills (complete with the 'tacked' clauses) or rejecting them and depriving the king of supply. Tacking was clearly seen as a last resort, to be used where reasoned argument had failed, but it was none the less regarded as justifiable. 'Since it can be no otherwise done,' declared Paul Foley in 1694, 'we must tack our grievances to our money bills; for we have just fears and grievances as long as we have a standing army' (7).

This remark was made during debates òn William's vetoing a triennial bill, during which some speakers effectively denied the king's right of veto. Robert Harley claimed that bills had rarely been vetoed in the past, especially when an abundant supply had been granted. 'One of the greatest crimes the minister can be guilty of is to persuade the king not to pass bills,' said Foley (7). Such remarks and the occasional use of tacking show that the Commons knew that they had the financial power to reduce the king to a cipher, if they used it systematically. But they did not. The threat in 1690 to withhold supply unless William dropped his opposition to the corporation bill came to nothing. Tacking was used only when a majority of MPs felt that it was absolutely necessary, that the Lords and king were opposing the Commons' wishes unreasonably. It was an occasional, almost desperate tactic, not a regular practice. The Lords disliked it, and if the Commons used it excessively the Lords were likely to delay or obstruct business which was important to the Commons. The king, too, could retaliate by using his veto.

Such practical considerations apart, many MPs had reservations about the propriety of tacking. Although they knew that their 'power of the purse' enabled them to force their wishes on the king, they lacked the will or the cohesion to use that power systematically. It is tempting to treat the Commons as an organism with a single mind and purpose. In fact, it comprised some five hundred individuals with varying interests and aptitudes. Some were concerned with local prestige or local economic interests, some were eager to solicit rewards for themselves and their kinsmen, but only a minority were interested in a 'political career'. MPs were unpaid. Long, regular sessions were a novelty which many disliked. Most still saw government as the king's business. They did not want the responsibility of policy-making and administration. They wanted to criticise what they saw as errors of policy or maladministration, especially where their class or personal interests were affected. They wanted, also, to criticise the misdeeds of ministers and courtiers and (in some cases) to thrust themselves forward as possible replacements. Such complaints and criticisms were essentially selective. MPs criticised particular policies and particular ministers and demanded changes of measures and of men. They attacked the misuse of executive authority but not the king's right to direct the executive, because they did not themselves want executive responsibilities. This was seen clearly late in 1689. After allegations of gross abuses in the provisioning of the army in Ireland, William asked the Commons to name persons to take over the job and to report on the state of the Irish forces. The House was embarrassed. Sir Thomas Littleton moved 'that it is too weighty for us to meddle with'. Sir Christopher Musgrave claimed that 'it was not the practice of your ancestors to recommend persons for the executive part. The king's council and generals are fittest, knowing the abilities and qualities of persons.' The House asked to be excused from nominating anyone and referred everything to 'His Majesty's great wisdom'. As Sir Edward Seymour explained a few days later: 'We have no part of the executive authority of the government, but we may advise the king.... The general scheme of the state of the nation is as much as we can represent to the king.... It is not in our power to remedy the miscarriages, but it is to represent them to the king to be remedied' (**7**). The Commons did not normally use their financial position to wrest power from the king, but did so if a sufficiently large majority felt sufficiently angry to exert sustained financial pressure. The growth of parties, however, threatened to change this. While the Commons remained little more than an agglomeration of individuals or small groups, it was hard to keep a majority together on any but the most emotive issues. The development of party issues and party discipline gave the leaders of the majority party something approaching a constant majority in the Commons, which they could then use to force their way into office. If the monarch would not employ them, they could make the House unmanageable. Taken to its logical extreme, this would have turned the monarch into the tool of the party leaders. Between 1705 and 1710 the Whig leaders used their control of the Commons to force Anne to dismiss her Tory advisers, to admit Whigs to office and to follow Whig policies [**doc. 38**]. As early as 1707 Anne had to resort to subterfuge to appoint two moderate Tory bishops. After 1715 the constant Whig majority in Parliament left the first two Georges with no choice but to appoint Whig ministers. Yet the crown's position was not as desperate as it seemed. There were limits to how far politicians could carry their obstruction: if they took it to the point of jeopardising the war effort, their followers might desert them. Not all politicians were fervent party men. Some great ministers, like Marlborough, Godolphin, Harley and Sunderland, put service to the crown before party. Career civil servants like William Lowndes served under ministries of any party complexion. Among the party men, some moderates, like the Duke of Somerset, were prepared to serve in mixed ministries. The party leaders were rarely so united that the crown could not play one off against another or rely on moderates rather than extremists − the Whig Junto's solidarity in 1705−10 was exceptional. After 1715 the Whigs' supremacy was so secure that they felt little need for unity. Had George I and II been more astute, their choice of possible ministers would have been wider than it was (**65**).

Thus after 1689 the crown's financial weakness gave the Commons the power to impose their will on the king, if they chose to do so. The growth of party divisions imparted greater cohesion to the House. Party leaders were thus better able to channel and exploit that power and to subject the crown to more sustained pressure, which affected all the crown's major prerogatives. The right to summon and dismiss Parliament at will was curtailed by the Triennial Act and by the need to continue each session until the year's money bills were completed. The king was commander-in-chief of the armed forces, but in 1697−8 William was forced to reduce the army to what he saw as suicidally small proportions. The king formulated foreign policy, but Parliament had to pay for war. Like his predecessors, William sometimes found it wise to lay treaties before Parliament (as in 1692), but he tried to keep Parliament (and his own ministers) ignorant of some of his negotiations. In 1701 the Commons declared themselves outraged upon discovering the secret partition treaty of 1698. This sense of outrage owed more to the Tory majority's hatred of the Whigs who had been William's ministers at the time of the treaty (and who had known nothing of it) than to a desire to take over foreign policy-making, but thereafter William was careful to keep the House informed and ask its advice. Finally, as we have seen, the monarch's right to choose his ministers still respected in theory, proved harder and harder to exercise in practice. MPs' suspicions of corruption and mismanagement could be exploited and channelled by politicians eager to do down their rivals. Even William reluctantly acknowledged the need to appoint ministers who could manage Parliament, even if he disliked them personally. Like Sunderland, he came in 1693−4 to accept that 'whenever the government has leaned to the Whigs it has been strong, whenever the other has prevailed it has been despised'. He also shared Sunderland's sorrow at this state of affairs: 'The Whigs make me weary of my life and I would give half of what I am worth that it were otherwise' (**81**).

Such pressures led to the decline of personal monarchy. William possessed exceptional ability and determination. His control of foreign policy was facilitated by his being able to use the Dutch diplomatic service. Relying on a few comparatively humble officials, he directed almost single-handed the administration of the army and, to a lesser extent, the navy. Yet even William, with all the prestige he enjoyed as England's saviour in 1688 and as the leader of the coalition against France, suffered numerous defeats and humiliations [**doc. 20**]. Political needs forced him to appoint men he despised — he would not even speak to Wharton, for example. Parliament rescinded his grants of Irish lands to Dutchmen and Huguenots, with cutting remarks about the rapacity of foreigners. Worst of all, William was forced to disband most of the army at a time when he believed that a renewal of the war was imminent, and to send home his Dutch guards (**20**). Anne has perhaps been underestimated by historians. If she lacked William's exceptional gifts, she was conscientious and determined, with clear views of her own. Her main concern was to win the war. She wished to maintain the toleration of 1689 while preventing further weakening of the Church. She was also determined to preserve the crown's prerogatives and to avoid domination by party politicians [**doc. 37**]. She clung to these principles in the face of ruthless and cynical pressure from those (not least the Duchess of Marlborough) who sought to take advantage of her sex and physical frailty [**doc. 38**]. Despite her efforts, however, her abilities were inferior to William's and she faced greater problems, with the intensification of party rivalries. As a result her defeats, especially at the hands of the Whig Junto, were more numerous (**58**).

George I and George II were less able monarchs than Anne. George I's resentment of the 'Tory' peace of 1713 and his acceptance of the Whig equation of Toryism and Jacobitism left him no choice but to rely on the Whigs, but the Whigs were not united. It said much for Walpole's skill as both a court and a parliamentary politician that he monopolised the two kings' favour for twenty years. His security of tenure and the Georges' mediocrity made it possible to carry on the government with less reference to the king's personal wishes. Decisions reached in cabinet were presented to the king as *faits accomplis*. Walpole was thus able to extract the maximum of political benefit from the crown's powers of patronage and to pursue policies at home and abroad that were congenial to independent backbench MPs. This mixture of patronage and policies gave Walpole a well-nigh unshakable hold on the Commons, which greatly strengthened his hand in dealing with the king (**83, 98**). Ministers' deference of expression and their care to win royal approval on sensitive issues, such as foreign policy or court and military appointments, does not alter the fact that in the last resort they held the whip hand. They might explain to George II (as to an obtuse pupil) that all they were doing was for his benefit, that without these necessary measures they could not get his business — in other words, supply — through the Commons [**docs. 39, 40**]. They might have genuine reservations about the propriety of cajoling or bullying the king. In the last resort, however, they could get their way by mass resignation. In 1746 the Pelhams and their followers resigned because the king would not follow their advice. The king's favourites, Lords Granville and Bath, tried to form a ministry but could not carry the Commons. George, therefore, had to take the Pelhams back on their own terms (**94**) [**doc. 41**]. The crown's effective power was not entirely destroyed. A king could still choose his ministers, but only from those enjoying the confidence of Parliament. George III was more determined than his grandfather and the fragmentation of political groups in the 1760s gave him (temporarily) a wider choice than usual. He made many suggestions on matters of detail but (as under George II) the broad lines of policy were laid down by his ministers, with his approval (**35**). With the re-emergence of ideological divisions and of a popular dimension to politics, the king's personal authority dwindled further. He could still refuse to employ certain individuals or to approve certain policies (as with George III and Catholic emancipation), but he was no longer responsible for formulating policy. He was little more than a chairman of a committee, which often asked his opinion for politeness' sake, but which reached major decisions without necessarily taking his views into account. When George III died, the monarch was well on the way to becoming a figurehead whose influence, such as it was, was mainly informal.

Because the monarch's personal power declined so much faster and so much more completely in practice than in theory, it is extremely difficult to pinpoint the stages in its decline. Clearly, however, the Glorious Revolution was of fundamental importance. Although the men of 1689 had not intended to deprive the king of effective power, they quite deliberately reserved to Parliament the financial leverage to ensure that that power would not be abused. On occasion (notably under William) the Commons as a whole felt sufficiently outraged to use that power to extort concessions from the king. Increasingly, however, it was the politicians who used their control of the Commons, a control strengthened by party ties, to force themselves and their followers into office and to force their policies on the monarch. They were then able to use this control over patronage and policies to strengthen their control over the Commons. In the early Hanoverian period, the main beneficiaries of the Revolution seemed to be the Whig oligarchs who exploited the legacy of the Revolution to dominate both the crown and Parliament (**97**). Not until new popular political issues challenged the politicians' direction of policy and economical reform eroded their powers of patronage did the Commons begin to realise their potential, and Britain begin to move hesitantly towards parliamentary democracy.

11 The Law and Local Government

Both the Bill of Rights and the 'heads of grievances' showed a particular concern with the misuse of the legal system, after the courts' harassment of Whigs and Dissenters in Charles II's last years and the crude pressure which James put on his judges. Such blatant interference with the processes of justice came to an end in 1689. Although before 1701 there was no law against the king's dismissing judges for political reasons, in practice William respected their independence. The Trials for Treason Act of 1696 removed some of the disadvantages suffered by the accused in such cases: they were now allowed counsel and a copy of the indictment; they could challenge up to thirty-five of those named as jurors; above all, two witnesses were now required for a conviction. Together with the Habeas Corpus Act of 1679 (temporarily suspended in 1689–90), these measures did much to secure the liberty of the individual against the state. Political trials did not come to an end, but it was not until the Jacobin trials of the 1790s that the courts were again used systematically against political dissidents.

The liberalisation was not universal, however. The Riot Act of 1716 made it lawful for troops to fire on rioters (or demonstrators) who failed to disperse after due warning: hitherto, soldiers who shot rioters were liable to find themselves indicted for murder. Moreover, if the law became more respectful of individual liberty, it also became far more severe in its defence of property. The number of offences carrying the death penalty increased from about fifty in 1689 to over two hundred in 1800. Most were offences against property − a pickpocket who stole a shilling could be hanged. Beggars or the mothers of illegitimate children could be flogged. After 1689 England enjoyed religious liberty, a comparatively free press and a large measure of political freedom, but infringements of the sanctity of property could be punished with a most unenlightened brutality.

This obsession with protecting property underlines the fact that the main beneficiary of the Revolution was the landed élite, whose members came increasingly to dominate politics in the generations after 1689, and hence gained most from the growth of political liberty. The new legislation protecting property was passed by a Parliament of landowners and enforced by landowners as magistrates. These landowner-magistrates now carried on local government with much less interference than in the past from the central government. Medieval, Tudor and early Stuart Parliaments had passed a mass of legislation to protect the interests of the poor and the consumer against greedy landlords, grain speculators and the worst effects of harvest failure. Many towns' market regulations gave local consumers precedence over outside dealers, even though the latter might be prepared to pay more. Some larger towns had municipal grain stocks, to be sold off below market rates in years of shortage. The object of such measures was to keep grain prices down, especially when dearth forced up prices. The poor laws were designed to supplement these preventive measures in years of crisis: they were not intended to be the sole source of relief for the poor.

After 1660 most earlier legislation remained on the statute book but the central government no longer pressed the local authorities to enforce it. The landed families who regained local office after 1660 showed less and less interest in protecting the poor and the consumer. The long Tudor inflation had stopped and food prices even showed a tendency to decline. At the same time, taxation on land was heavier — often much heavier — than before 1640. Real wages, which had fallen drastically during the price rise, began to recover. The emphasis of legislation was now on keeping prices up. A supply bill of 1673 provided for a bounty on corn exports, if prices at home fell below a certain level. The provision was only temporary, but corn bounties became a regular feature of economic policy after 1689. By encouraging exports they reduced the risk of a glut and of a collapse of prices at home.

Thus by the end of the seventeenth century, government economic policy had come to favour the producer rather than the consumer. Clearly economic conditions were now much less favourable to producers than they had been a century earlier. Even so, it is hard to avoid the conclusion that the landed élite had become self-centred, more concerned with its own interests and less with those of the poor, while the crown would not or could not mitigate the effects of this selfishness. The problem of poverty certainly did not go away. With the abandonment of the old preventive measures, the whole burden was thrown on the poor rate, whose yield rose from perhaps £250,000 a year in the mid-seventeenth century to around £700,000 at the end (**112**). In other ways, too, the central government increasingly left local magistrates to their own devices. Apart from the occasional investigation of Papists, the crown showed no interest in religious nonconformity. It expected JPs to ensure that taxes were collected and it knew that it could rely on them to maintain law and order. For the rest, its interest in local government was mainly political. Local offices were seen primarily as instruments of political patronage and were milked of every drop of electoral advantage. In the boroughs little Whig oligarchies entrenched themselves in power. In the counties JPs ruled with greater independence than ever before. In the areas of law and local government, perhaps more clearly than anywhere else, one sees that the main benefit of the Revolution was reaped not by the people at large but by the small landed élite and a smaller oligarchy of politicians.

81

12 Parties and the Working of Politics

One problem constantly facing the historian of politics is that of motivation. How far are people concerned with power and profit and how far with issues of principle? If it is naive to see parliamentary debates as abstract discussions of political philosophy, it is usually over-cynical to dismiss them as a smokescreen of rhetoric behind which politicians pursued sordid material ambitions. There were times when political issues apparently counted for little. In the 1750s, according to Namier 'the nation was at one in all fundamental matters, and whenever that happy but uninspiring condition is reached, Parliamentary contests lose reality and unavoidably change into a fierce, though bloodless, struggle for office' (**91**). Whether or not this was true of the 1750s (and some historians would deny it), it was certainly not true of the generation after 1689, as Namier himself recognised. The nation was divided on a number of important issues of principle, which complicated and gave an added ferocity to the perennial struggles of politicians to gain power and do down their rivals. The pursuit of power and the pursuit of principle were far from incompatible. A deep commitment to a particular policy could increase one's eagerness to achieve the power one needed in order to pursue that policy. Men seeking honourable ends were quite capable of using dishonourable means in pursuit of their goal. The pursuit of power and of principle could thus reinforce one another [**doc. 45**] and the men of William's and Anne's reigns managed to combine strong ideological commitment with a large measure of greed, corruption and cynicism.

Before considering the nature of party divisions, a brief functional analysis of the Commons would be helpful. By far the largest element consisted of 'backbenchers' – landowners, merchants, lawyers, army officers and minor officials. Such men had many reasons for entering Parliament, ranging from family tradition to a desire to make profitable business or professional contacts. Some were sturdily independent, others eagerly sought rewards for themselves and their families. The one thing they had in common was that they did not see themselves as candidates for major office — they lacked the time, the interest, the connections, the experience or the ability. The second group, much smaller, were the London-based career civil servants. Most were men of lukewarm (or non-existent) party loyalties, professionals for whom election to Parliament was part of the job. They spoke mainly on the affairs of their own departments and normally defended official policy. Thirdly, there were the politicians, men who had achieved or who wanted major office, who possessed (or thought they possessed) talent as administrators or debaters. In office, they usually defended ministerial policy. Out of office, they denounced the folly and corruption of the existing administration. Often, however, a ministry (especially a mixed ministry) was divided within itself. On such occasions it was common for ministers to attack their supposed colleagues [**doc. 46**].

The politicians and civil servants provided most of the regular speakers in the Commons. The politicians provided the articulate leadership in the party conflicts of the day. They could achieve little, however, without backbench support. Even if their motives were factious and selfish, therefore, they had to couch their arguments in terms of principle and the public good. These arguments would have been ineffectual had not the principles to which they appealed been widely shared. With that in mind, let us consider the two axes along which men divided in this period — Court against Country and Whig against Tory.

These two divisions did not necessarily coincide. The Commons would not divide along the same lines on a 'Country' issue as they would on a 'party' issue. These were, moreover, different *kinds* of division. 'Court–Country' divisions centred on attitudes to the executive. The 'Court' in any division consisted of those siding with the king's ministers on that particular issue; the 'Country' of those against them. More fundamentally, the 'Country' expressed distrust of those in power. The approach of most 'Country' MPs was essentially negative. They did not want power themselves, they just criticised the abuses of those who exercised it. Many were profoundly suspicious of the corrupt ways of the capital, of courtiers and civil servants. There was thus a certain nebulousness about 'Court–Country' divisions. If some criticised the king's ministers year in, year out, with sturdy consistency, others' attitudes varied, depending on who was in power and the issue in question. Traditional backbench ideals of independent MPs, making up their minds on each issue according to its merits, prevented

'Court–Country' divisions from attaining the rigidity and formality of a party system. Too often a maverick 'Country' MP decided that this time the ministers were in the right or allowed personal obligations to a minister to change his mind. Too often the pull of patronage outweighed the appeal of principle, or the 'detested names' of Whig and Tory might prevail.

The division between Whig and Tory was different in kind. The core of the 'Court' comprised those in power for the time being. The 'Country' mostly did not want power. Whigs and Tories, however, both eagerly sought power in order to implement their party programme [**doc. 45**]. While it was not always possible to label an MP as 'Court' or 'Country' – many flitted from one to the other – it was far easier to classify an individual as 'Whig' or 'Tory'. The surviving division lists show that most MPs supported one party consistently on the major issues which divided Whig from Tory, especially under Anne (**29**). Between 1690 and 1700 the predominant political issues divided 'Court' and 'Country', with 'party' issues surfacing comparatively rarely. Under Anne, on the other hand, the major issues were party issues and contemporaries could predict how men would vote with an accuracy that had not been possible in the 1690s. The rage of party permeated all aspects of English life. From parliament and parliamentary elections, party feelings reached out into municipal politics and appointments to local office. There were Whig and Tory clubs, theatres, race-meetings, even doctors. The party identities thus created had a definition and a permanence never acquired by 'Court' and 'Country'. They also acquired an organisation, in the constituencies, in the political clubs and taverns of London and in both Houses of Parliament, where the Whigs especially built up an effective system of party whips and discipline (**65, 97, 109**).

Whether 'Court–Country' or 'Whig–Tory' divisions predominated depended mainly on the nature of the major issues at any given time. The Convention Parliament was very much concerned with the legacy and animosities of the 1680s, so 'Whig–Tory' divisions predominated. The 1690s saw various new issues, which owed much to the war and the strains it imposed, and which mostly set 'Country' against 'Court'. First, MPs complained of the unprecedented – some said unwarranted and insupportable – burden of taxation. They claimed that much was wasted or embezzled and that the figures they were given were designed to mislead. Some reeled off statistics (their origin and accuracy alike uncertain) which purported to show that the government had plenty of money and that king and taxpayer were being cheated by the administration [**doc. 42**]. Second, fears grew that the government's greater financial and patronage resources posed a real threat to Parliament's independence [**doc. 43**]. 'Country' MPs responded with the Triennial Act and a series of bills designed to exclude placemen of various types from the Commons. The total exclusion of placemen in the Act of Settlement was unrealistic — it would have made it impossible for the House to receive any accurate information about finance or administration — and it was repealed before it could take effect. Certain categories of revenue officers were excluded, however, and others had to seek re-election after accepting office (**76**). Linked to this question of the crown's influence was the resentment of a largely landed parliament at the rise of the monied interest. Bankers and stockjobbers, it was believed, were less worthy of trust than landed men. In times of national peril, they could take their gold and flee. The landed men could not. Their wealth was, literally, a part of England. Many believed that landownership, over the generations, inculcated an integrity and public spirit not found in those whose wealth came from speculation and usury. To stop monied men buying their way into Parliament, an Act of 1710 (never effectively enforced) laid down that county MPs should have a minimum income from land of £600 a year and the representatives of boroughs one of £300.

A third object of 'Country' anxiety was the standing army, which might enable the crown to break through the restrictions on its power imposed since 1689 and to levy money at will. William had long been suspected, in Holland and in England, of absolutist ambitions. When peace was signed in 1697, he had on foot an army of about sixty thousand, similar in size to Cromwell's and three times as large as James II's. It was argued that standing armies were found only in absolutist states, whose rulers depended on coercion and not on the love of their people. England, surrounded by sea, had less need than most of such an army: the navy, backed by a citizen militia, should suffice [**doc. 44**]. The 'Country' element in Parliament therefore used the power of the purse to force William to cut the army to around six thousand men.

A final feature of the 'Country' mentality was dislike of foreigners. William was an alien king, who spent each summer abroad and made little effort to make himself agreeable to the English [**doc. 20**]. At first he relied mainly on Dutchmen, Huguenots and Germans to command his armies, thinking them more experienced and trustworthy than most English officers. This annoyed the Commons.

'Englishmen naturally love their country and will not willingly destroy their country', declared Sir Peter Colleton in 1692. 'Foreigners cannot have that affection for England' (**7**). The Commons demanded that in future only British-born subjects should be commissioned as officers. A similar chauvinism was apparent in the debates on William's Irish land grants. In 1699 the Commons resolved that all foreigners (except Anne's husband, Prince George) should be excluded from William's counsels and a similar provision was included in the Act of Settlement.

It might seem that 'Country' sentiment was an inchoate and negative expression of backbench anger, but that would not be entirely true. Attacks on mismanagement focussed on individual ministers and were usually led by politicians, often those ministers' nominal colleagues: 'I believe what is done is rather designed against persons than to rectify things', remarked Seymour (**13**). This was especially apparent within mixed ministries. In 1692 the Whig politicians Wharton and Montagu led a series of attacks on the secretary of state, the Tory Earl of Nottingham. They accused him of mismanaging naval affairs and of disloyalty, on the grounds that he had opposed declaring the throne vacant and making William king in 1689 [**doc. 46**]. One should not, however, argue from this that 'Country' issues were raised only to promote personal or party ends, or that simple-minded backbenchers were constantly manipulated by unscrupulous politicians. 'Country' sentiment had a vitality and rationale of its own, which cut across party lines. If its main emphasis was negative, it was not purely destructive, as was shown by the Commissions of Accounts of the 1690s. From early in the reign Harley, Foley and others complained of the difficulty of obtaining reliable figures to use in assessing how much money the Commons should vote. 'It concerns us to give the king a supply', said Foley in 1690, 'but it concerns us as much not to give more than is necessary. We have strange accounts of the revenue. I hope our case is not so bad as is represented;... let us have a fair account' (**7**). William at this time favoured producing such accounts, which would show how inadequate his revenue was. For much the same reason, some older 'Country' MPs were against it. 'I would enter upon accounts no further than to supply the present occasion', declared William Garroway in November 1689. 'The deeper we entered on accounts, the deeper was always the charge. I have ever found it' (**7, 87**). Such objections were overcome, however, and at the end of 1690 the Commons named the nine MPs who were to serve on the Commission of Accounts for the following year.

Most of the nine were Whigs, but the commission included the formidable 'Country' spokesman and staunch Tory, Sir Thomas Clarges, who co-operated with men of Whiggish origins like Foley, Harley and Colleton in investigating financial mismanagement and in trying to overcome the obstruction and evasion of civil servants. If the commission unearthed few major scandals, its very existence acted as a deterrent. Its reports enabled MPs to offer better-informed criticism of the crown's financial demands and to prune the annual estimates for the armed forces. Its reports also served a constructive purpose. They helped mitigate the monumental ignorance of many backbenchers about money matters and about the true cost of the war. The commission thus deserves some credit for the Commons' increasingly constructive approach to both taxation and borrowing during the 1690s (**45, 69, 86**). Its leaders used their expertise constructively as well as destructively. In 1692, the Commons complained about subsidies which William had promised to pay to Savoy and Hanover. Harley and Foley thereupon carried a proposal to include them under the general heading of 'hospitals, contingencies and extraordinary charges' (**13**).

The Commission of Accounts was a striking expression of a developing 'Country' mentality, which threatened in the 1690s to supersede the divisions of Whig and Tory. The Commission lapsed in 1697 after the exclusion in 1696 of three Tories who refused to subscribe the Association, which not only included a promise to defend William against assassins, but styled him 'rightful and lawful' king. The next year the Whig ministers sought to pack the commission with their nominees, whereupon the Commons failed to renew it (**69**). The possibility of there emerging a 'Country' party always depended on there being no strong 'Whig—Tory' issues to cut across 'Country' loyalties. In 1700—1702, however, the party issues of the 1680s again came to the fore, albeit in modified forms, and the chances of a new political alignment were doomed. Even so, the preponderance of 'Country' issues in the 1690s had one lasting effect on party divisions. Before 1689 Whigs had been suspicious of the crown's power and influence — an essentially 'Country' outlook. The Tories, fearful of revolt and republicanism, had emphasised the crown's authority. James's misconduct and William's usurpation forced them to reappraise their position. In Sunderland's splendidly sarcastic phrase 'It was very true that the Tories were better friends to monarchy than the Whigs were, but then His Majesty was to consider that he was not their monarch' (**81**). Tories like Clarges resisted William's being made king and did their utmost to limit his powers. In so doing, they found they had much in common with old-style 'Country' Whigs like Foley who had little time for the younger Whigs of the Junto — Somers, Wharton, Montagu — who were eager for office and not scrupulous about their methods. The co-operation of Tories and Country Whigs in the 1690s did not lead to the formation of a new Country party, but it ended with many erstwhile Whigs (like Harley) severing their links with Whiggery and throwing in their lot with the Tories. From the Court–Country battles of the 1690s emerged an enlarged and revitalised Tory party (**49, 97**).

Such a transformation was possible only because the Whigs had always been a motley coalition, held together by insistence on Exclusion (**73**). With the exclusion from the throne of James and of all Catholics in 1689, the Whigs' original *raison d'être* disappeared, although the succession question re-emerged after the death of the Duke of Gloucester. However, during the battle over exclusion the parties had begun to develop conflicting ideologies and differing stances on other questions of principle. These differences of ideology and principle survived the Revolution and were to some extent transformed by it. They were to determine the shape of politics in the Convention Parliament and in the reign of Anne.

The first major difference between the parties concerned the nature of monarchy. To the Tories, monarchy and its attributes were divinely ordained and obedience to it was a sacred duty. To the Whigs, it was a traditional institution whose powers could be limited, if that seemed essential for the common good. While avoiding any clear exposition of a right to resist the monarch's commands, Whigs generally assumed that the subject's duty of obedience was not unconditional and could be overridden by the right of self-preservation. We have seen how the Tories were embarrassed by James's misrule and his replacement by William. They disliked what had happened, but could see no alternative: they certainly did not want James back. 'The utmost necessity', said Sir Henry Goodricke 'made me break my oath to king James' (**7**). Most found it difficult to take an oath of allegiance to William and Mary, even though the oath omitted the usual reference to their being 'rightful and lawful' monarchs [**doc. 47**]. Their scruples were exploited by the Whigs, who sought to appropriate the sole credit for the Revolution and to argue that only the Whigs were truly committed to William's régime and so worthy of trust. They argued that anyone who had opposed declaring the throne vacant should not be on the Council and tried repeatedly to strengthen the oath of allegiance. The Assassination Plot of 1696 brought about a great revulsion of feeling in William's favour and proved a godsend to the Whigs. By forcing Tories to subscribe an Association to defend William's person (which included the phrase 'rightful and lawful'), they drove some out of office. Most Tories, however, ground their teeth and subscribed the Association and, in 1701, an oath abjuring the Pretender. Although many Tories allowed their enthusiasm for divine right and non-resistance one last fling under Anne, they were moving towards a new definition of non-resistance, in which obedience was due to established authority or to the monarch in Parliament rather than to the monarch alone [**doc. 48**]. Meanwhile the Whigs, who had never been entirely happy about avowing the subjects' right of resistance, came under Anne to appreciate that those most likely to resist established authority were the Jacobites. They too began to stress the subject's duty to obey the powers that be. After 1714 the Tories' attachment to divine right was moribund and Whig and Tory views on the nature of monarchy and the question of resistance became almost indistinguishable (**42, 80**).

The differences between Whig and Tory attitudes to monarchy had originally focussed on the succession. For Tories, God had established the hereditary succession and men could not alter it. To the Whigs, hereditary right should normally be respected, but could be overridden if the national interest required it. These rival views were clearly evident in the debates on the change of ruler in 1689, after which the question remained dormant until Gloucester died in 1700. The Tories reluctantly agreed that the Electress of Hanover was the next heir, but found the prospect distasteful: her hereditary claim was far weaker than William's had been. Small wonder, then, that the eyes of some Tories turned to James's son, the Old Pretender: although a Papist, he was also a Stuart. As the Hanoverian succession loomed nearer, more and more Tories indulged in the fantasy that the Pretender might abandon his Catholicism and so qualify for the throne. Such fantasies were eagerly exploited by the Whigs, who raised the succession question whenever they could, especially in the last years of Anne's reign. They argued constantly that the Tories were Jacobites and that only the Whigs were truly loyal to the Protestant succession. This was not true. As one Jacobite remarked bitterly in 1715, the Tories were 'never right hearty for the cause till they are mellow, as they call it, over a bottle or two... they do not care for venturing their carcases any further than the tavern' (**10**). If the Tories were emotionally drawn to the Stuarts, reason led the majority to accept the Hanoverian succession. As in 1688−9 and in 1701, forced to choose between the Protestant religion and the hereditary principle, the great majority of Tories chose the former. However, a few did opt for the Pretender and many others accepted the Hanoverians with such bad grace that for another generation Whig politicians were able to make political capital out of the allegation that the Tories were Jacobites.

Another major difference between the parties, also dating back to the Exclusion Crisis, concerned the Church. The majority of Tories were High Churchmen and believed that religion and morality had been trampled underfoot since the Toleration Act. They raged against occasional conformity, trying to make it illegal by tacking a clause against it to the supply bill in 1704. Over the next few years their rage increased, as the Junto proposed to admit Dissenters to the universities, to grant toleration to Dissenters in Ireland and to naturalize thousands of Calvinists from the Palatinate. The last straw was the Whigs' impeachment of Dr Henry Sacheverell, a parson whose prejudices against Whiggery made up in vehemence what they lacked in coherence. He was impeached for a sermon in which he denied that resistance had occurred in 1688−9, but his prosecution was seen as yet another example of the Whigs' vindictiveness against the Church. In London a High Church mob smashed Dissenting meeting houses and the homes of leading Whigs; it was stopped by troops on its way to attack the Bank (**67**). Sacheverell was convicted, but the Tories won the propaganda battle and the Lords imposed only a light punishment. The trial showed clearly the great strength of High Church sentiment and the unpopularity of Dissent.

The last major party issue was foreign policy. In the wars of 1689−97 and 1702−13, the Whigs argued that the French could be defeated only by a land campaign and that it was vital for England that Louis XIV should not overrun the Low Countries. The Tories claimed that land wars were unnecessary and expensive, that they benefited England's continental allies far more than England, and that national interests could best be served by a war against France's trade and colonies [**doc. 49**]. The war of the Spanish succession was initially popular, thanks to Marlborough's victories, but later disillusionment set in. War taxation was high and the harvest of 1709 was the worst for many years. In these circumstances, many could not understand the Whigs' refusal to negotiate with Louis (who was offering generous terms) until such time as his grandson had been expelled from Spain, particularly as the Spaniards did not want him to go and the allies lacked the military resources to drive him out. The Tories won much popular support for their attack on the war and for their argument that it had become a device whereby the monied interest grew rich on the taxes paid by landowners and consumers [**doc. 31**].

The popularity of the Tories' stand on the Church and foreign policy was demonstrated by their crushing victories in the general elections of 1710 and 1713, which did much to substantiate their claim to be the natural majority party. To Bolingbroke, the Tories represented the true English interest while the Whigs represented sectional and often alien interests: England's foreign allies, the monied men, the Dissenters [**doc. 45**]. A decade earlier the Tory William Bromley had complained 'how those who are the smaller part of the nation have made themselves formidable and terrible to the greater' (**103**). Elections under the Triennial Act were freer and more frequent than ever before. Elections became a regular occurrence, which had not been the case in Charles II's reign, which saw only four general elections, three of them in 1679–81. Neither William nor Anne interfered systematically in elections, because they wished neither party to win a crushing victory. The electorate, meanwhile, grew larger than at any time before 1832. Inflation reduced the value of property qualifications for voting, especially in the counties. In many boroughs the uncertainties of the franchise were exploited by whichever party stood to gain from an enlarged electorate. As a result the electorate played a larger part in political life than ever before. In many constituencies it was too large to be bribed or browbeaten and had to be wooed by the two parties. Electors were influenced as much as the ruling élite by the great issues of the day. Most constituencies had two members and the great majority of electors voted for two Whig or two Tory candidates, rather than one of each. Electors also changed their minds according to the issues of the moment: the large and independent electorate of London, for instance, voted in four Whigs in 1708 and four Tories in 1710 (**97, 109**).

Under Anne the Tories were usually more successful than the Whigs in appealing to the electors. Only in 1708 did the Whigs win a clear victory; they were humiliated in 1710 and 1713. The Tories' great assets were resentment of war taxation and commitment to the Church, of which only the second remained important throughout the reign. It is hard now to think of the Church of England as militant, but it had massive popular support under Anne and its clergy ruthlessly attacked the Dissenters and Whigs: on the eve of the Sacheverell riots, one London parson preached on the text: 'Break their teeth, O God, in their mouths.' The Tories exploited a growing hostility to Dissent, a hostility all the greater when those Dissenters were immigrants, like the 'poor Palatines'. Against this all the Whigs had to offer was anti-Popery and the claim that the Tories were Jacobites. Their victory in 1708 followed an attempted Jacobite rising in Scotland and their triumph in 1715 owed much to the fear that the Tories wished to bring in the Pretender, a fear soon strengthened by the flight to France of Bolingbroke and Ormonde. The Whigs had a virtual monopoly of George I's favour, but could not trust the electors to vote them in again. They began to extend techniques which they had already begun to use, designed to ensure a constant Whig majority in the Commons. Great Whig magnates like Newcastle and Devonshire enlarged their empires of pocket boroughs. Every scrap of local patronage was used to the Whigs' electoral advantage. Political considerations governed the appointment of customs and excise men, of army officers in garrison towns, of bishops and canons in cathedral cities. The Commons' committee of elections and privileges showed (as always) a strong partisan bias in deciding election disputes. Above all, the Septennial Act of 1716 ensured that in future MPs need face the electors only every seven years rather than every three. As a result, election results ceased to reflect swings of public opinion. Even after the furore of the Excise Crisis of 1733, Walpole's majority was almost unchanged in 1734. The Tories continued to do well in the counties and the more open boroughs, but the Whigs controlled enough of the small boroughs (and the forty-five Scottish MPs who sat at Westminster after the Union) to ensure an unassailable majority. In many constituencies, Tories ceased to stand as they had no chance of winning: some even defected to the Whigs. Contests became rarer. Only in a minority of constituencies was the electoral vigour of Anne's reign sustained (**66, 83, 97**).

It is one of history's many ironies that so soon after the Revolution provoked (in part) by James II's attempts to pack Parliament, the electoral system should have been perverted, more subtly but more effectively, by Walpole. The Bill of Rights' ringing declaration 'that election of Members of Parliament ought to be free' must have sounded hollow in the 1730s. By then, the energy and the willingness to innovate which were so apparent in the 1690s had become overlaid by conservatism and complacency. The Whig party, which had once stood for 'clean' government and religious liberty, now raised political 'corruption' to a level of unparalleled sophistication and quietly forgot the interests of the Dissenters (**80**). Both old-fashioned radical Whigs and maverick Tories like Bolingbroke denounced Walpole for betraying 'Revolution principles' and wondered if they were really any better off as a result of the Revolution: the corrupting influence of money seemed to rule all (**82**). Such jeremiads were unnecessarily pessimistic. Walpole depended as much on pursuing policies acceptable to backbench MPs as on the use of patronage. If he and the Pelhams met with so little opposition, this was in part a tribute to their understanding of the moods and prejudices of the Commons, which enabled them to avoid contentious issues, and to their willingness to back down if, by chance, such issues arose. (This was the case with both the excise scheme of 1733 and the Jew Bill of 1753.) Such an approach was made easier by the demise of the great issues of Anne's reign. The great majority of Tories accepted George I's accession and in time lost their sentimental fondness for the Stuarts. A long period of peace laid to rest the animosities aroused by the war of 1702–13. Even the Church ceased to be an issue: the Whig leaders of the later 1710s abandoned their predecessors' fondness for antagonising the Churchmen.

If the Commons temporarily became less responsive to the electorate, the crown was becoming more dependent on those who could manage the Commons. When the electors' influence over the Commons' composition was restored in the nineteenth century, it was to prove far easier to force the people's wishes on the monarch than had been the case in the seventeenth. If the likes of Montesquieu and Voltaire exaggerated the liberty enjoyed by Englishmen and the merits of the British constitution, their writings are a salutary correction to Bolingbroke's pessimism and a reminder that, by continental standards, England was a free country with a liberal political system. It had solved by consent the problem of mobilising the nation's resources for war, a problem the French crown had failed to solve by compulsion. Galling though it was for the French, England managed to combine its eccentric constitution with a power in world affairs out of all proportion to its size.

There is no indication that the men of 1688–9 had planned this. Their main aim had been preservation – indeed, self-preservation – against the threat of 'Popery and arbitrary government'. Few had any conception of the feasibility of progress or of constitution-building. Most were suspicious of change and agreed to alter the constitution only when this seemed necessary to prevent other, more drastic, changes. The changes of 1688−9 were limited, uncoordinated and pragmatic. They were not given coherence by the sort of ruthless logic which underlay France's administrative restructuring in the 1790s or the *Code Napoléon*. And yet, oddly, they worked. They left intact those elements of the medieval constitution (Parliament above all) which preserved traditions of reciprocity and consent and which, in many countries, were crushed with the advent of absolutism. Whereas the rigidity of absolutism could often be overcome only by violence, the flexibility of the British constitution allowed it to adapt to changing expectations and to the perception of new needs. If such a constitution, with all its surviving anomalies, smacks more of pragmatism than of rigorous logic, that in itself could be seen as typically English. This pragmatism, this preference for adapting the old rather than sweeping all away and starting afresh, was a feature of the Glorious Revolution. If we ask why England never underwent a revolution comparable to the French and Russian revolutions, perhaps we should conclude, as Macaulay did, that one major reason was that England had undergone a bloodless revolution at the end of the seventeenth century.

13   Postcript: Ireland and Scotland

It is inevitable that any study of the Glorious Revolution should focus on England. It was much the richest and most populous of William III's three kingdoms and its wealth and military might enabled it to impose its will on the other two. The element of military force was obvious in Ireland. James II had restored civil and military power to those Catholics of English descent who had once run the country, which revived hopes of an independent Ireland. When William invaded England, these Catholics tried to extend their sway over the whole country, but were thwarted by the Protestants of Londonderry and Enniskillen. Soon James arrived from France and an English army landed in Ulster, but it was not until July 1690 that James's and William's armies met at the Boyne. Militarily it was no contest. James fled to France, but the Irish continued to fight, surrendering at Limerick in October 1691 on honourable terms (which were not fully implemented) (**106**).

The Irish surrender completed the establishment of the Protestant ascendancy in Ireland. Thereafter Catholics were excluded from political power and lost most of what little land they had left. It was this which gave the Boyne its great symbolic significance in Protestant eyes: it was the one striking victory of the war. For the time being, Irish Catholic nationalism was broken. Jacobite risings in Scotland and England aroused no echo in Ireland. For most of the eighteenth century, expressions of national feeling were confined to the Protestant élite, who complained, much as the American colonists did, of their stifling subjection to the mother country. Only in the 1790s was there a revival of Catholic nationalism, which led directly to the Union of 1800.

English rule in Ireland had always depended on the sword and the Revolution reaffirmed Ireland's subordination to England. Scotland had never been conquered by the English. The union of crowns of 1603 had left Scotland's institutions intact and English influence within Scotland depended on winning the co-operation of Scottish magnates. The rewards of such co-operation were great, but the magnates were usually at odds with one another, which gave

Scottish politics a built-in instability. James's attempts to advance the fortunes of Scottish Catholicism had been thwarted by the fewness of the Scottish Catholics. Early in 1689 an assembly of Scottish nobles and gentry asked William to summon a Convention, which met in March. Like its English counterpart, this drew up a 'Claim of Right' and invited William and Mary to accept the Scottish crown. In August Jacobite resistance was broken, at the battle of Dunkeld, but William found it difficult to rule Scotland. None of the great magnates could control the Scottish Parliament on his own, yet they would not work together. After ten years of unstable parliamentary politics, English ministers saw the advantages of joining the Scots Parliament to that of England: a single Parliament, at Westminster, would be far easier to manage. The Act of Settlement added a second incentive to union. The Scottish Parliament was in no hurry to agree to the Hanoverian succession, hoping for concessions from England in return. Its dilatoriness raised the prospect that the Old Pretender might become king of Scotland when Anne died.

The Act of Union of 1707 has aroused strong emotions in Scotland. Some see it as corrupt in intention and in execution, designed to establish a bloc of venal Scottish MPs at Westminster and pushed through by bribery and intimidation. In fact, the terms of the Union were far from unfavourable. The Scots were to retain their own legal system and their Presbyterian Church, re-established in 1689. The customs union between the kingdoms helped to alleviate the depression of Scottish trade. Ambitious Scottish politicians could hope to prosper in the richer pastures at Westminster. Many Scots accepted the need for some sort of union, but Scottish opinion was deeply divided on the terms they were offered, the divisions being complicated by the endemic factionalism of Scottish politics. It is clear that the terms of union contained much that was acceptable to a variety of opinions and although bribery was used, it is unlikely to have been decisive: if it was allegedly so effective in 1707, why had bribery failed since 1689 to impose any discipline on the Edinburgh Parliament? (**64, 101**). The Union came to seem far less desirable in retrospect, partly because the British government failed to respect some of the original terms, but more because of the indifference shown by British ministers towards Scottish interests after 1707 (**84**). This created the impression that the Union had led to the submerging of Scotland's identity and interests and its subordination to its larger neighbour, an impression which survives undiminished to this day.

Part Four: Documents

document 1
Anti-Catholicism

document 1

This typical Exclusionist pamphlet describes the horrors which would allegedly ensue if England had a Catholic ruler.

First, imagine you see the whole town in a flame, occasioned this second time by the same Popish malice which set it on fire before. At the same instant, fancy that amongst the distracted crowd you behold troops of Papists ravishing your wives and daughters, dashing your little children's brains out against the walls, plundering your houses and cutting your own throats by the name of heretic dogs. Then represent to yourselves the Tower playing off its cannon and battering down your houses about your ears. Also, casting your eye towards Smithfield, imagine you see your father, or your mother, or some of your nearest and dearest relations, tied to a stake in the midst of flames, when with hands and eyes lifted up to heaven they scream and cry out to that God for whose cause they die, which was a frequent spectacle the last time Popery reigned amongst us... . Your trading's bad, and in a manner lost already, but then the only commodity will be fire and sword, the only object women running with their hair about their ears, men covered with blood, children sprawling under horses' feet and only the walls of houses left standing...

C. Blount, 'An Appeal from the Country to the City' (1679), reprinted in *State Tracts*, 2 vols, London, 1689–92, vol. I, pp. 401–2.

document 2
Persecution of Dissenters

Usually Charles II's government relied on the normal machinery of law to harass Dissenters, but on this occasion it considered using regular troops, as Louis XIV did against the Huguenots.

The king being given to understand that a dangerous conventicle continues to be kept at Oldbury, about four miles from Birmingham and that several hundreds resort thither, many whereof are armed, has ordered two troops of dragoons to be quartered in the neighbourhood to be assistant in suppressing the said dangerous meeting and apprehending the offenders, whom he would have proceeded against with all severity according to law.

Earl of Sunderland to Sir Charles Holt, *Calendar of State Papers, Domestic, 1684–5,* p. 237.

document 3

The attack on the borough charters

In this letter Sir John Knight, the Tory sheriff of Bristol, gives the secretary of state his reasons why the borough's charter should be confiscated.

That the corporation have forfeited their charter is apparent from the following particulars:

1. By the charter and former practice, the Common Council was chosen yearly by the Mayor and Sheriffs, afterwards by the Mayor and two Aldermen, but now it is run into a practice that once a Common Councilman and ever so and the members are chosen by the majority of the Council.

2. The Common Council ought by the charter to be but 43... but ever since 1660 the Council have exceeded 43 and are 53....

3. The Aldermen ought to be chosen out of those who have been Mayor, but this has not been done of late.

4. The gaol delivery ought to be held once a year. This has been of late frequently neglected to the great prejudice of the keeper and the prisoners. Many other practices might be added, as suffering conventicles, putting men out of the Council, denying justice in gaol delivery and Quarter Sessions, &c.

Calendar of State Papers, Domestic, 1682, pp. 239–40.

document 4

'Political justice'

The procedure in treason trials was always heavily weighted against the accused. Jeffreys' language in the trial of Alice Lisle in 1685 differed only in degree from that used from the bench in the political trials of 1681–4.

Blessed God! What is the way that this devil of sedition comes to bewitch people to such a height, when Almighty God had so lately delivered us from the misery and confusion of a civil war? It is that way surely, we find it but too plain, when he had always found very successful the practice of saintship, conscience and that glorious name, religion. What religion can it be?... Good God! That we should live in such an age, when men call God to assist and protect them in a rebellion... Jesus God! That ever we should have such a generation of vipers amongst us, that can plunge themselves into the most horrid impieties and yet think to escape confusion here and purchase a crown of glory hereafter...

Kenyon (**11**), p. 435.

document 5

James II's political creed

Unlike James I, James II was no philosopher, but while in exile he drew up some papers of advice for his son, which give an insight into his views on kingship.

Kings being accountable for none of their actions but to God and themselves ought to be more cautious and circumspect than those who are in lower stations and as 'tis the duty of subjects to pay true allegiance to him and to observe his laws, so a king is bound by his office to have a fatherly love and care of them.... Consider you come into the world to serve God Almighty and not only to please yourself and that by Him kings reign and that without His particular protection nothing you undertake can prosper.... Therefore preserve your prerogative, but disturb not the subjects in their property nor conscience, remember the great precept, Do as you would be done to, for that is the law and the prophets...

J.S. Clarke (ed.), *Life of James II*, 2 vols, London, 1816, vol. II, pp. 619–21.

document 6

James and the succession

Although many feared that James planned to change the succession in favour of a Catholic, this letter (written to a leading Catholic extremist, who supported such a change) shows that he had no such intention.

Not only could it never enter my head to think of changing it, but I know well that it is not in my power to do it, even if a Pope and a Parliament joined with me. For where the crown is hereditary (as it is in these kingdoms, thanks be to God) His Almighty power alone can dispose of it, not only the hearts of kings but their crowns being in His hands...

James to Albeville, c. 29 March 1687, Archives des Affaires Étrangères, Paris, Correspondance Politique, Angleterre 164, fol. 28.

document 7
James's reasons for becoming a Catholic

In 1687 James wrote to his daughter Mary, urging her to follow his example and become a Catholic. This is the main reason he gave for his own conversion.

Surely it is only reasonable that this Church, which has a constant succession from the time of the apostles to the present, should be more in the right than those private men who, under the pretext of reformation, have been the authors of new opinions.... It was this consideration which principally led me to embrace the communion of the Roman Church, there being no other which claims, or can claim, infallibility, for there must necessarily be an infallible Church, or otherwise what Our Saviour said cannot be and the gates of Hell would prevail against her...

M. Bentinck (ed.), *Lettres et Mémoires de Marie, Reine d'Angleterre*, The Hague, 1880, pp. 7–8.

document 8
The French Ambassador's view of James's intentions

Barrillon knew James very well and naturally did not share his subjects' fear and hatred of Catholicism and absolutism. He was quite sure that James's main aim was to promote his religion.

As far as I can see, the King is sincerely concerned to leave [the Catholics] in security after his death, because the ardour with which he seeks the repeal of the penal laws is more for their sake than his own, and although he often says, when talking of the revocation of the Test oath, that he would risk everything rather than allow his subjects to take an oath by which they declare him an idolater, it is also a question of the security of the Catholics, whose lives and safety will be at the mercy of his successor and of Parliament if these laws are still in being on the day of his death.

Barrillon to Louis XIV, 11/21 July 1687, Public Record Office, PRO 31/3/171.

document 9

Godden v. Hales

This test case was designed to secure a ruling from the judges upholding the dispensing power.

We think we may very well declare the opinion of the court to be that the king may dispense in this case; and the judges go upon these grounds:
1. That the kings of England are sovereign princes.
2. That the laws of England are the king's laws.
3. That therefore 'tis an inseparable prerogative in the kings of England to dispense with penal laws in particular cases and upon particular necessary reasons.
4. That of those reasons and those necessities the king himself is sole judge...

Kenyon (**11**), p. 439.

document 10

The dispensing power condemned

In the trial of the Seven Bishops, Mr Justice Powell made it clear that he thought James's use of the dispensing power had gone far beyond what the judges had considered acceptable in 1686.

Gentlemen, we must consider what they [the bishops] say is illegal in it. They say, they apprehend the declaration is illegal because it is founded upon a dispensing power which the king claims, to dispense with the laws concerning ecclesiastical affairs. Gentlemen, I do not remember any case in all our law... that there is any such power in the king and the case must turn upon that. In short, if there be no such dispensing power in the king, then that can be no libel which they presented to the king, which says that the declaration, being founded upon such a pretended power, is illegal.... I can see no difference, nor know of one in law, between the king's power to dispense with laws ecclesiastical and his power to dispense with any other laws whatsoever. If this be once allowed of, there will need no Parliament; all the legislature will be in the king, which is a thing worth considering and I leave the issue to God and your consciences.

Kenyon (**11**), p. 445.

document 11

Instructions to election agents, 1688

These agents, many of them former Exclusionists, had two tasks: to provide the central government with detailed information about local politics and personalities and to influence as many electors as possible in favour of repealing the penal laws and Test Acts.

1. You shall make the king's declaration [of indulgence] the chief subject of your discourse with such persons as you shall think fit to speak with....

6. You are to make acquaintance with the leading, active and interested men in the county, or in the towns and corporations, who are inclinable to abrogate the penal laws for religion and the tests, and engage them to improve their interest for effecting it.

7. You are to inform yourself (as privately as may be) whether the persons proposed to be chosen, by the list given you, be right-principled and so disposed to part with the laws as may be depended on.

8. You are to inform yourself whether the regulations made in the respective corporations have been of proper persons for His Majesty's service.

9. You are to inform yourself who are the electors in the respective corporations and boroughs, and by what manner elections are made, who influences them, and who are fittest to be chosen in those places where none are yet proposed.

10. You are to inform yourself of the behaviour of the officers of the several branches of His Majesty's revenue in relation to elections, whether they promote His Majesty's interest as they ought to do, and further what in them lies the repeal of the penal laws and tests.

11. [You are] to acquaint yourselves with the preachers of the Dissenting congregations and to encourage them to employ their

interest for the abrogating those laws and tests....

12. You are to inform yourself of some fit person in each corporation with whom a correspondence may be held for the knowledge of the true state of the same, and to whom books and pamphlets may be sent, to disperse them for the people's better information...

Kenyon (**11**), pp. 509−10.

An election agent at work

document 12

Finding most of the gentry, whether Tory or Whig, unwilling to agree to support the repeal of the penal laws and Test Acts, some agents resorted to threats and intimidation, as shown by this extract from the diary of Sir John Knatchbull of Kent.

About the end of April following [1688] an old acquaintance came to me to speak with me about the business of repealing the penal laws and test.... He said that people were generally misinformed and therefore prepossessed with His Majesty's bigotry, that he was no such manner [of man]...that neutrality was suspected both at court and in the country, that I was looked upon as one very stiff in the negative by the king, that I was represented as one particularly obstinate in this point; and that the king's eye was upon me as one likely to influence the country, & c.... I told him that I had given him an answer the night before, which was that I gave my lord Tenham [the lord lieutenant], and desired him to insist no more on it: he was very warm and urgent with me in this business, saying that I was morose and obstinate...not having sufficiently considered the consequence of things...

P.C. Vellacott, 'The Diary of a Country Gentleman in 1688', *Cambridge Historical Journal*, vol. II, 1926, pp.52−3.

Propaganda aimed at the Dissenters

document 13

Of all the pamphlets which aimed to exploit and increase the Dissenters' unease at being asked to support the repeal of the Test Acts in return for James's toleration, Halifax's Letter to a Dissenter *was perhaps the most effective.*

Consider that notwithstanding the smooth language which is now put on to engage you, these new friends [the Catholics] did not make you their choice but their refuge. They have ever made their first courtships to the Church of England, and when they were rejected there they made their application to you in the second place.... This alliance between liberty and infallibility is bringing together the two most contrary things that are in the world. The Church of Rome doth not only dislike the allowing liberty, but by its principles it cannot do it....

Whatever may be told you at this very hour, and in the heat and glare of your present sunshine, the Church of England can in a moment bring clouds again and turn the royal thunder upon your heads, blow you off the stage with a breath, if she would give but a smile or a kind word; the least glimpse of her compliance would throw you back into the state of suffering and draw upon you all the arrears of severity which have accrued during the time of this kindness to you. And yet the Church of England, with all her faults, will not allow herself to be rescued by such unjustifiable means, but chooseth to bear the weight of power rather than lie under the burden of being criminal... .

Besides all this, you act very unskilfully against your visible interest if you throw away the advantages of which you can hardly fail in the next probable revolution [James's death and Mary's accession]...

Halifax (**8**), pp. 106, 113–4, 116.

document 14

England in the spring of 1688

In this letter, dated 12 April, Halifax assured William that all James's schemes were doomed to failure. William did not share his optimism and a few weeks later began to prepare his invasion. (Note also Burnet's pessimism: see **doc. 16**). *The birth of James's son in June was to transform the situation: now that he had a Catholic heir, much of the urgency which Halifax describes disappeared.*

There hath been little that is new this great while, since either the old methods have continued, or else what appeareth to be new is at least not strange, being produced by a natural consequence and therefore to be reasonably expected and foreseen. In some particulars, to men at a distance the engine seemeth to move fast, but by looking nearer one may see that it doth not stir upon the whole matter so that here is rapid motion without advancing a step, which is the only miracle that Church hath yet showed to us. Every attempt turneth back upon them. They change the magistracy in the corporations and still for the worse as to their own designs. The irregular methods have spent themselves without effect; they have run so fast that they begin to be out of breath, and the exercise of extraordinary powers, both ecclesiastical and civil, is so far from fixing the right of them that men are more united in objecting to them. The world is still where it was, with this only difference, that it groweth every day more averse to that which is endeavoured to be imposed upon them. The very Papists who have estates act unwillingly, like pressed men, and have such an eye to what may happen in a revolution that their present advantages hardly make amends for their fears.... Being thus discouraged by their ill success in their attempts, some say they are altering their schemes, and not finding their expectations answered by the Dissenters, they have thoughts of returning to their old friends, the High Churchmen; but the truth is, the Papists have of late been so hard and fierce upon them that the very species of those formerly mistaken men is destroyed.... In the meantime, the men at the helm are certainly divided amongst themselves...

Halifax (**8**), pp. 338−9.

William's attitude to repeal

document 15

In his efforts to win support for the repeal of the Test Acts, especially from the Dissenters, James was especially eager to persuade William and Mary (who seemed certain to succeed him) to come out publicly in favour of repeal. When approached by Albeville, James's ambassador at the Hague, William made it clear that he supported repeal of the penal laws, but not of the Test Acts. He told Albeville

that he had never heard or read in any history of two dominant religions at the same time in one kingdom or state; so that the Roman religion could not become dominant without the king's breaking the laws and his own promises and without (he feared) one day causing disorders which would imperil the monarchy; as for himself, he could not consent to, or approve, these proceedings of the king's and the Marquis d'Albeville would find the Princess of

Orange in the same sentiments and as firmly resolved as himself; that it would be better to assure the Catholics of a reasonable liberty for the present and the future than to expose them to persecution and perhaps to extirpation; for himself, he had never approved and would never approve of persecution for religion or of forcing consciences; that he would maintain the Catholics in an honest liberty, as they have in this country, but he could never agree or consent to allow them to become dominant...

Albeville to d'Avaux, *c.* 17 May 1687, Public Record Office, FO 95/573.

document 16
Burnet's thoughts at the end of 1687

Gilbert Burnet's History of my own Time *is frequently well-informed and perceptive. Between 1686 and 1688, however, he was in exile in Holland. His assessment of what was happening in England rested in large part on inaccurate rumour, speculation and wishful thinking. Many of his misconceptions were shared by William.*

The extremity to which the king has driven matters will throw the nation into great confusions which it will be very hard to manage. For either the nation will lose heart and then a multitude will become the feeblest thing in the world; or, if the vigour of the subjects is still kept up, it will be hard to govern this and keep it from breaking out upon great provocations, chiefly if a force is put upon the elections of Parliament men, which strikes at all.... If the king's ill conduct throws the nation into such a violent fermentation, then a rebellion that prospers will turn to a commonwealth, and if it is subdued it will put all things in the king's hands.... A war at home of any continuance will naturally bring over a French army, in whose hands the king will put such places as are in his power...

Burnet (**3**), pp. 261–2.

document 17
William's declaration

Designed to appeal to Tories as well as Whigs, this gave a catalogue of James's misdeeds (blamed on evil counsellors, not the king himself) and proposed the one remedy on which all could agree — a free Parliament.

We cannot any longer forbear to declare that, to our great regret, we see that those counsellors who have now the chief credit with the king have overturned the religion, laws and liberties of those realms and subjected them, in all things relating to their consciences, liberties and properties, to arbitrary government....

But to crown all, there are great and violent presumptions inducing us to believe that those evil counsellors, in order to the carrying on of their ill designs, and to the gaining to themselves the more time for the effecting of them...have publishéd that the queen hath brought forth a son; though there hath appeared, both during the queen's pretended bigness, and in the manner in which the birth was managed, so many just and visible grounds of suspicion, that not only we ourselves but all the good subjects of those kingdoms do vehemently suspect that the pretended Prince of Wales was not born by the queen....

We cannot excuse ourselves from espousing their [the kingdoms'] interests in a matter of such high consequence; and from contributing all that lies in us for the maintaining, both of the Protestant religion and of the laws and liberties of those kingdoms...to the doing of which we are most earnestly solicited by a great many lords, both spiritual and temporal, and by many gentlemen and other subjects of all ranks. Therefore it is, that we have thought fit to go over to England and to carry over with us a force sufficient, by the blessing of God, to defend us from the violence of those evil counsellors...we now think fit to declare, that this our expedition is intended for no other design but to have a free and lawful Parliament assembled as soon as is possible...

Williams (**18**), pp. 10−11, 15.

document 18
William's demands, 9 December 1688

These make it clear that William was prepared to agree to a settlement whereby James remained king.

1. That all Papists and such persons as are not qualified by law be disarmed, disbanded and removed from all employments civil and military.

2. That all proclamations which reflect on us or [any that] have come to us, or declared for us, be recalled and that if any persons for

having so assisted us have been committed, that they be forthwith set at liberty.

3. That for the security and safety of the City of London, the custody and government of the Tower be immediately put into the hands of the said City.

4. That if His Majesty should think fit to be in London during the sitting of the Parliament, that we may be there also with an equal number of guards, or if His Majesty shall be pleased to be in any place from London, at whatever distance he thinks fit, that we may be at a place of the same distance. And that the respective armies do remove from London forty miles. And that no further forces be brought into the kingdom.

5. That for the security of the City of London, and their trade, Tilbury Fort be put into the hands of the said City.

6. That to prevent the landing of French or other foreign troops, Portsmouth may be put into such hands as by Your Majesty and us shall be agreed on.

7. That some sufficient part of the public revenue be assigned us for the support and maintenance of our forces, till the meeting of a free Parliament.

Halifax (**9**), vol. II, pp. 29–30.

document 19

William insists on being made king

Burnet tells how William broke the deadlock between the two Houses about offering the crown to William as well as Mary.

After a reservedness that had continued so close for several weeks that nobody could certainly tell what he desired, he called for the Marquis of Halifax, the Earls of Shrewsbury and Danby and some others to explain himself more distinctly to them.... He said no man could esteem a woman more than he did the Princess; but he was so made that he could not think of holding anything by apron strings; nor did he think it reasonable to have any share in the government unless it was put in his person and that for term of life; if they did think to settle it otherwise...he would go back to Holland and meddle no more in their affairs.... He could not resolve to accept of a dignity, so as to hold it only for the life of another: yet he thought that the issue of Princess Anne should be preferred in the succession to any issue that he might have by any other wife than the Princess.

Burnet (**2**), vol. III, pp. 395−6.

document 20

Burnet's assessment of William

Burnet knew William well. Here he tries to explain why, although William was a great European figure, he was neither appreciated nor liked by the English.

His strength lay rather in a true discerning and a sound judgment than in imagination or invention: his designs were always great and good: but it was thought he trusted too much to that and that he did not descend enough to the humours of his people, to make himself and his notions more acceptable to them. This, in a government that has so much of freedom in it as ours, was more necessary than he was inclined to believe: his reservedness grew on him, so that it disgusted most of those who served him: but he had observed the errors of too much talking, more than those of too cold a silence. He did not like contradiction nor to have his actions censured: but he loved to employ and favour those who had the arts of complaisance, yet he did not love flatterers....

He knew all foreign affairs well, and understood the state of every court in Europe very particularly: he instructed his own ministers himself, but did not apply enough to affairs at home....

His indifference as to the forms of church-government and his being zealous for toleration, together with his cold behaviour towards the clergy, gave them generally very ill impressions of him.... He loved the Dutch, and was much beloved among them: but the ill returns he met from the English nation, their jealousies of him and their perverseness towards him, had too much soured his mind, and had in a great measure alienated him from them, which he did not take care enough to conceal, though he saw the ill effects this had upon his business....

I considered him as a person raised up by God to resist the power of France and the progress of tyranny and persecution.... After all the abatements that may be allowed for his errors and faults, he ought still to be reckoned among the greatest princes that our history, or indeed that any other, can afford.

Burnet (**2**), vol. IV, pp. 562−7.

document 21

Locke's political theory

Locke's Two Treatises of Government *were published, anonymously, early in 1690. Their purpose was 'to establish the throne of...King William' and 'to justify to the world the people of England'. These extracts illustrate some major points in the argument.*

(a) The Original Compact

Men being...by nature all free, equal and independent, no one can be put out of his estate and subjected to the political power of another without his own consent. The only way whereby any one divests himself of his natural liberty and puts on the bonds of civil society is by agreeing with other men to join and unite into a community, for their comfortable, safe and peaceable living one amongst another, in a secure enjoyment of their properties and a great security against any that are not of it.... When any number of men have so consented to make one community or government, they are thereby presently incorporated and make one body politic, wherein the majority have a right to act and conclude the rest.

Locke (**12**), pp. 374–5.

(b) Political power as a trust

The legislative being only a fiduciary power to act for certain ends, there remains still in the people a supreme power to remove or alter the legislative when they find the legislative act contrary to the trust reposed in them. For all power given with trust, for the attaining an end, being limited by that end, whenever that end is manifestly neglected, or opposed, the trust must necessarily be forfeited, and the power devolve into the hands of those that gave it, who may place it anew where they shall think best for their safety and security.

ibid., p. 413.

(c) The dissolution of government

Besides this overturning from without [by conquest], governments are dissolved from within. First, when the legislative is altered.... When any one, or more, shall take upon them to make laws, whom the people have not appointed so to do, they make laws without authority, which the people are not therefore bound to obey...being in full liberty to resist the force of those who, without authority, would impose anything upon them....

When such a single person or prince sets up his own arbitrary will in place of the laws which are the will of the society, declared by the legislative, then the legislative is changed...whoever introduces new laws not being thereunto authorized by the fundamental appointments of the society, or subverts the old, disowns and overthrows the power by which they were made and so sets up a new legislative...

ibid., pp. 455–7.

In these and the like cases when the government is dissolved, the people are at liberty to provide for themselves by erecting a new legislative, differing from the other by the change of persons, or form, or both, as they shall find it most for their safety and good...

ibid., p. 459.

Here 'tis like, the common question will be made, who shall be judge whether the prince or legislative act contrary to their trust?... To this I reply, the people shall be judge; for who shall be judge whether his trustee or deputy acts well and according to the trust reposed in him but he who deputes him and must, by having deputed him, have still a power to discard him when he fails in his trust?...

ibid., p. 476.

The end of government is the good of mankind, and which is best for mankind, that the people should be always exposed to the boundless will of tyranny or that rulers should be sometimes liable to be opposed, when they grow exorbitant in the use of their power and employ it for the destruction and not the preservation of the properties of their people?...

ibid., p. 466.

document 22

Tory adherence to principle, 1689

The following was one of the arguments which the Lords drew up for use in the conference with the Commons on 6 February. It expresses the Tory majority's dogmatic attachment to the hereditary principle and also, much less explicitly, their desire to avoid making William king.

Although the Lords have declared that the king has deserted the government, and thereupon they have made application to the Prince of Orange to take upon him the administration of the government and thereby to provide for the peace and safety of the kingdom; yet there can be no other inference drawn from thence, but only that the exercise of the government by King James II was ceased; so as that the Lords were and are willing to secure the nation against the return of the said king into this kingdom; but not that there was either such an abdication by him or such a vacancy in the throne, as that the crown was thereby become elective.... No act of the king alone can bar or destroy the right of his heirs to the crown; and therefore...if the throne be vacant of King James II, allegiance is due to such person as the right of succession does belong to.

Lords Journals, vol. XIV, p. 117

document 23
Whig pragmatism, 1689

In these speeches from the conference between the Houses on 6 February, the Whig spokesmen for the Commons based their case not on broad, abstract constitutional principles but on the pragmatic argument that a vacuum existed at the head of the government and that it was up to the Convention to fill it.

Sir John Maynard: I am sure, if we be left without a government, as we find we are (why else have we desired the Prince to take upon him the administration?) sure we must not be perpetually under anarchy.... All they [the Commons] mean by this matter is to provide a supply for this defect in the government brought upon it by the late king's maladministration. And I do say again, this provision must be made: and if it be, that would not make the kingdom perpetually elective...

Sir Thomas Lee: I would ask this question, whether upon the original contract there were not a power preserved in the nation to provide for itself in such exigencies? That contract was to settle the constitution as to the legislature...so we take it to be; and it is true that it is a part of the contract, the making of laws and that those laws should oblige all sides when made; but yet so as not to exclude this original constitution in all governments that commence by compact, that there should be a power in the states to make provision in all times and upon all occasions for extraordinary cases and necessities, such as ours now is...

Maynard: If we look but into the law of nature (that is above all human laws) we have enough to justify us in what we are now a-doing, to provide for ourselves and the public weal in such an exigency as this...

Parliamentary History (**14**), vol. V, pp. 89, 100, 103.

document 24
The post-revolution constitution: contract theory

This passage is taken from The Revolution Vindicated, *published in 1689 to justify the Revolution. It gives a fuller description of the 'original contract' than any in the surviving debates of the Convention, but ends up (as usual) in seeing the contract as implicit in the Ancient Constitution.*

By the Original Contract was meant the agreement that had always been between the kings and people of England, that the government should be a legal government. When this agreement was first made, and the particular form and nature of it in its infancy, are things as obscure as the beginning of governments; but vestiges of it are to be found as far back as we can go, and it may be traced down through the whole history of England, and of the many wars and revolutions that have happened, to make it good, and in which kings have suffered expressly for breaking it. Besides, the thing is obvious everywhere in the frame of the government, for how came it to be a bounded limited monarchy, but that bounds and limits were agreed on? And whensoever this was first done, the Original Contract had then its rise and birth.

Kenyon (**80**), p. 43.

document 25
A mixed and balanced constitution

*The following extract from a Whig pamphlet from 1697 shows how little the traditional view of the constitution, as a mixture of monarchy, aristocracy and democracy, had changed. Compare this with Charles I's answer to the Nineteen Propositions (Kenyon (**11**), pp. 21–2).*

Our constitution is a limited mixed monarchy, where the king enjoys all the prerogatives necessary to the support of his dignity and the protection of his people and is only abridged from the power of injuring his own subjects... . Lest the extraordinary power intrusted in the crown should lean towards arbitrary government, or the tumultuary licentiousness of the people should incline towards a democracy, the wisdom of our ancestors hath instituted a middle state, viz. of nobility, whose interest it is to trim this boat of our commonwealth, and to screen the people against the insults of the prince and the prince against the popularity of the Commons, since if either extreme prevail so far as to oppress the other, they are sure to be overwhelmed in their ruin... . The excellence of this government consists in the due balance of the several constituent parts of it, for if either one of them should be too hard for the other two, there is an actual dissolution of the constitution; but whilst we can continue in our present condition, we may without vanity reckon ourselves the happiest people in the world.

J. Trenchard and W. Moyle, *An Argument Showing that a Standing Army is Inconsistent with a Free Government*, 1697, reprinted by The Rota, Exeter, 1971, pp. 2–3.

document 26
Heads of grievances, 7 February 1689

The first list of grievances, drawn up on 2 February, made no distinction between heads confirming old laws and those which required fresh legislation: see Horwitz (69), pp. 367–8. The first part of this document, slightly modified, became part of the Declaration of Rights and, after further amendments, the Bill of Rights, for which see Williams (18), pp. 26–33. The second part was dropped.

The said Commons so elected, being now assembled in a full and free representative of this nation, taking into their most serious consideration the best means for attaining the ends aforesaid, do in the first place (as their ancestors in like case have usually done) for the vindicating and asserting their ancient rights and liberties, unanimously declare,

That the pretended power of dispensing or suspending of laws, or the execution of laws, by regal authority, without consent of Parliament, is illegal;

That the commission for erecting the late court of commissioners for ecclesiastical causes and all other commissions and courts of like nature are illegal and pernicious.

That levying of money for or to the use of the crown, by pretence of prerogative, without grant of Parliament, for longer time, or in other manner, than the same is or shall be granted is illegal.

That it is the right of the subjects to petition the king and all commitments and prosecutions for such petitioning are illegal.

That the raising or keeping of a standing army within the kingdom in time of peace, unless it be with consent of Parliament, is against law.

That the subjects which are Protestants may provide and keep arms for their common defence.

That election of Members of Parliament ought to be free.

That the freedom of speech and debates or proceedings in Parliament ought not to be impeached or questioned in any court or place out of Parliament.

That excessive bail ought not to be required; nor excessive fines imposed; nor cruel and unusual punishments inflicted.

That jurors ought to be duly impanelled and returned; and jurors which pass upon men in trials for high treason ought to be freeholders.

That all grants and promises of fines and forfeitures of particular persons before conviction are illegal and void.

And that for the redress of all grievances and for the amending, strengthening and preserving of the laws, Parliaments ought to be held frequently and suffered to sit... . And towards the making a more firm and perfect settlement of the said religion, laws and liberties, it is proposed and advised...that there be provision by new laws...to the purposes following, viz.

For repealing the Acts concerning the militia and settling it anew;

For securing the right and freedom of electing members of the House of Commons, and the rights and privileges of Parliaments, and members thereof, as well in the intervals of Parliament as during their sitting;

For securing the frequent sitting of Parliaments;

For preventing the too long continuance of the same Parliament;

For securing universities, cities and towns corporate and boroughs and plantations against Quo Warrantos and surrenders and mandates and restoring them to their ancient rights;

None of the royal family to marry a Papist;

Every King and Queen of this realm at the time of their entering into the exercise of their regal authority, to take an oath for the maintaining the Protestant religion and the laws and liberties of this nation; and the coronation oath to be altered;

For the liberty of Protestants in the exercise of their religion; and for uniting all Protestants in the matter of public worship, as far as may be;

For regulating constructions upon the statutes of treasons, and trials and proceedings and writs of error in cases of treason;

For making judges' commissions *quamdiu se bene gesserint*; and ascertaining and establishing their salaries, to be paid out of the public revenue only; and for preventing their being removed and suspended from the execution of their offices, unless by due course of law;

For better securing the subjects against excessive bail in criminal cases and excessive fines and cruel and unusual punishments;

For reforming abuses in the appointing of sheriffs and in the execution of their office;

For securing the due impanelling and returning of jurors and preventing corrupt and false verdicts;

For taking away informations in the Court of King's Bench;

For regulating the Chancery and other courts of justice, and the fees of officers;

For preventing the buying and selling of offices;

For giving liberty to the subjects to traverse returns upon habeas corpuses and mandamuses;

For preventing the grants and promises of fines and forfeitures before conviction;

For redressing the abuses and oppressions in levying the hearth money;

And for redressing the abuses and oppressions in levying and collecting the excise.

Commons Journals, vol. X, pp. 21–2

document 27

Debate on the King's revenues, 27 February 1689

Clarges and Seymour were both Tories; their speeches reflect Tory disenchantment with William, but also a concern (shared with many Whigs) not to repeat the mistakes of 1660 and 1685, when the king was granted enough revenue to enable him to make himself independent of Parliament.

Sir Thomas Clarges: I would have the monarch and the people in mutual confidence or else there is no safety to either. I think we ought to be cautious of the revenue, which is the life of the government, and consider the two last reigns. It seems, by the king's declaration, we are out of danger of falling into the misfortunes of the two last governments. If you give this revenue for three years, you will be secure of a Parliament. I doubt not the people of England, when they meet here and have good execution of their laws and are in security and safety; 'tis an unreasonable supposition that the people will not aid him according to his occasions. And I move, that the revenue may be settled for three years.

Sir Edward Seymour: What you settle on the crown I would have so well done as to support the crown and not carry it to excess. We may date our misery from our bounty here. If King Charles II had not had that bounty from you, he had never attempted what he had done.

Grey (**7**), vol. IX, pp. 123, 125.

Burnet on the King's revenues

document 28

Like the Commons, William knew that the revenue was the key to the constitutional settlement. Burnet recorded William's anger at the Commons' determination to deny him an adequate revenue.

He expressed an earnest desire to have the revenue of the crown settled on him for life: he said he was not a king till that was done: without that, the title of a king was only a pageant. And he spoke of this with more than ordinary vehemence: so that sometimes he said, he would not stay and hold an empty name, unless that was done...he was sure that the worst of all governments was a king without treasure and without power. But a jealousy was now infused into many, that he would grow arbitrary in his government, if he once had the revenue; and would strain for a high stretch of prerogative as soon as he was out of difficulties and necessities.

Burnet (**2**), vol. IV, pp. 60–61.

document 29
High Church retreat on comprehension

In 1688, leading High Churchmen discussed with certain Dissenters ways of making the Church of England service more acceptable to Presbyterians. By January 1689 the Church's leaders no longer felt any need to woo the Dissenters and feared that William favoured the Dissenters and disliked the Church. As a result, they began to have second thoughts about comprehension, as Clarendon found when he visited Archbishop Sancroft.

He said he knew well what was in their petition,* and he believed every bishop in England intended to make it good, when there was an opportunity of debating those matters in Convocation; but till then, or without a commission from the king, it was highly penal to enter upon church matters; but however he would have it in his mind and would be willing to discourse any of the bishops or other clergy thereupon, if they came to him; though he believed the Dissenters would never agree among themselves with what concessions they would be satisfied. To which Dr Tenison replied, he believed so too, that he had not discoursed with any of them upon this subject; and the way to do good was not to discourse with them, but for the bishops to endeavour to get such concessions settled in Parliament, the granting whereof (whether accepted or not by the Dissenters) should be good for the Church.

Clarendon Correspondence (**4**), vol. II, p. 240.

document 30
Arguments for and against comprehension

A committee of divines was ordered to draw up a list of possible changes to the Prayer Book, to be laid before Convocation.

We had some very rigid, as well as very learned, men among us: though the most rigid either never came to our meetings or they soon withdrew from us... . They thought too much was already done for the Dissenters in the toleration that was granted them...that the altering the customs and constitution of our church to gratify a peevish and obstinate party was like to have no other effect on them,

---

* The Seven Bishops' petition had declared a willingness 'to come to such a temper [with the Dissenters] as shall be thought fit when that matter shall be considered and settled in Parliament and Convocation'.

but to make them more insolent; as if the Church, by offering these alterations, seemed to confess that she had been hitherto in the wrong... . But in answer to all this it was said that if by a few corrections or explanations we offered all just satisfaction to the chief objections of the Dissenters, we had reason to hope that this would bring over many of them... . Ritual matters were of their own nature indifferent and had always been declared to be so: all the necessity of them arose only from the authority in church and state that had enacted them. Therefore it was an unreasonable stiffness to deny any abatement or yielding in such matters in order to the healing the wounds of our church... . The toleration now granted seemed to render it more necessary than formerly to make the terms of communion with the Church as large as might be; that so we might draw over to us the greater number from those who might now leave us more safely...

Burnet (**2**), vol. IV, pp. 55−7.

document 31
The rise of the monied interest: Bolingbroke in 1709

In this letter to Lord Orrery, Bolingbroke states, forcefully and lucidly, the Tory claim that the war had destroyed the old pre-eminence of landed wealth and created a new form of wealth, at once morally inferior and politically subversive.

We have been twenty years engaged in the two most expensive wars that Europe ever saw. The whole burden of this charge has lain upon the landed interest during the whole time. The men of estates have, generally speaking, neither served in the fleets nor armies, nor meddled in the public funds and management of the treasure.

A new interest has been created out of their fortunes, and a new sort of property which was not known twenty years ago is now increased to be almost equal to the terra firma of our island. The consequence of all is, that the landed men are become poor and dispirited. They either abandon all thoughts of the public, turn arrant farmers and improve the estates they have left; or else they seek to repair their shattered fortunes by listing at court, or under the heads of parties. In the mean while those men are become their masters, who formerly would with joy have been their servants. To judge therefore rightly of what turn our domestic affairs are in any respect likely to take, we must for the future only consider what the temper of the Court and of the Bank is.

Holmes and Speck (**10**), pp. 135–6.

document 32
A Low Churchman's creed: Thomas Papillon

A merchant of Huguenot descent, Papillon adhered firmly to the Calvinist tradition shared by French Huguenots and English Puritans. Writing in the 1690s, he used 'Tory' and 'Whig' where a decade or so later one would have referred to 'High Church' and 'Low Church' — but by then the Low Church was becoming predominantly Latitudinarian.

The kingdom of England is made up of Papists and Protestants. The Protestants are divided, and of late years distinguished by the names of Tories and Whigs. Under the name of Tories is comprehended all those that cry up the Church of England in opposition to the Churches of Christ in foreign parts, that press the forms and ceremonies more than the doctrines of the Church, which are sound and Scriptural; and that either in their own practice are swearers, drunkards or loose in their conversation, or do allow of and are unwilling such should be punished, but give them all countenance, provided they stickle for forms and ceremonies and rail against and endeavour to discountenance all those that are otherwise minded.

Under the name of Whigs is comprehended most of the sober and religious persons of the Church of England that sincerely embrace the doctrines of the Church, and put no such stress on the forms and ceremonies, but look on them as human institutions, and not as the essentials of religion, and are willing that there might be a reformation to take away offence, and that desire that all swearing, drunkenness and ungodliness should be discountenanced and punished, and do own the foreign Protestant Churches as Churches of Christ, and hold communion with them:- As also all dissenters of the several persuasions are included under this title... .

[Some allege that the Whigs] would totally abolish episcopacy. This may be said of some Dissenters, but cannot be said of those called Whigs in general; for this action will best agree with a moderate episcopacy; and when such are in place as promote true religion and piety, the Church will flourish and the Clergy will be reverenced. But when the essentials of religion are not upheld and countenanced, to wit, truth in doctrine and holiness of conversation, but the stress is laid on forms and ceremonies, and all stigmatized and suppressed that come not fully up to them, however good and godly soever...this will bring a disparagement on the episcopal government, and especially if the bishops shall interest themselves so far in civil affairs as to interpose their ecclesiastical power to over-rule the votes of the people in the choice of their representatives.

A.F.W. Papillon, *Memoirs of Thomas Papillon of London, Merchant,* Reading, 1887, pp. 374—6.

document 33
The demand for the recall of Convocation, 1697

Francis Atterbury was one of the most militant of the High Church clergy. His Letter to a Convocation Man *stated clearly why High Churchmen thought the Church was in danger in the 1690s.*

In plain English, then, I think if ever there was need of a Convocation, since Christianity was established in this kingdom, there is need of one now: when such an open looseness in men's principles and practices and such a settled contempt of religion and the priesthood have prevailed everywhere; when heresies of all kinds, when scepticism, deism and atheism itself overrun us like a deluge; when the Mosaic history has by men of our own order been cunningly undermined and exposed, under pretence of explaining it; when the Trinity has been as openly denied by some as the Unity of the Godhead sophistically opposed by others; when all mysteries in religion have been decried as impositions on men's understandings, and nothing is admitted as an article of faith but what we can fully and perfectly comprehend; nay, when the power of the Magistrate and of the Church is struck at, and the indifference of all religions is endeavoured to be established by pleas for the justice and necessity of an universal toleration, even against the sense of the whole legislature. At such a time and in such an age, you and I, Sir, and all men that wish well to the interests of religion and the state cannot but think that there is great need of a Convocation.

Holmes and Speck (**10**), p. 116.

document 34
The Latitudinarian outlook: John Tillotson

This extract from one of Tillotson's sermons illustrates a central theme of Latitudinarianism — that God is kind and undemanding (unlike the severe, vengeful God of traditional Puritanism).

Is it not really desirable to every man that there should be such a Being as takes particular care of every one of us, and loves us, and delights to do us good, as understands all our wants and is able and willing to relieve us in our greatest straits when nothing else can?... Is it not every man's interest that there should be such a Governor of the world as really designs our happiness and hath omitted nothing that is necessary to it, as would govern us for our advantage, and will require nothing of us but what is for our good, and yet will infinitely reward us for the doing of that which is best for ourselves?... And we have reason to believe God to be such a Being, if he be at all... .

One of the great prejudices which men have entertained against the Christian religion is this, that it lays upon men heavy burdens and grievous to be borne, that the laws of it are very strict and severe, difficult to be kept and yet dangerous to be broken... . For the removal of this prejudice I have chosen these words of the apostle, which expressly tell us the contrary, that the commandments of God are not grievous... . Upon this account it will be requisite to take some pains to satisfy the reason of men concerning this truth, and if possible make it so evident that those who are unwilling to own it may yet be ashamed to deny it. And methinks I have this peculiar advantage of the argument that I have now undertaken, that every reasonable man cannot but choose to wish me success in this attempt, because I undertake the proof of that which it is every man's interest that it should be true...

Sykes (**111**), p. 151.

document 35
Statutory limitations on the crown: the Act of Settlement, 1701

Although the immediate purpose of this Act was to ensure that Anne would be succeeded by the House of Hanover, its full title was 'An Act for the further limitation of the crown and better securing the rights and liberties of the subject'. It reflected the widespread belief that William had sacrificed the English to foreign interests and the fear that a future German king might try to do the same.

And whereas it is requisite and necessary that some further provision be made for securing our religion, laws and liberties, from and after the death of his Majesty and the princess Anne of Denmark...be it enacted...

That whosoever shall hereafter come to the possession of this crown, shall join in communion with the Church of England, as by law established.

That in case the crown and imperial dignity of this realm shall hereafter come to any person, not being a native of this kingdom of England, this nation be not obliged to engage in any war for the defence of any dominions or territories which do not belong to the crown of England, without the consent of Parliament.

That no person who shall hereafter come to the possession of this crown, shall go out of the dominions of England, Scotland or Ireland, without consent of Parliament.

That from and after the time that the further limitation by this act shall take effect, all matters and things relating to the well governing of this kingdom, which are properly cognizable in the privy council by the laws and customs of this realm, shall be transacted there, and all resolutions taken thereupon shall be signed by such of the privy council as shall advise and consent to the same.

That after the said limitation shall take effect as aforesaid, no person born out of the kingdoms of England, Scotland or Ireland, or the dominions thereunto belonging (although he be naturalized or made a denizen, except such as are born of English parents) shall be capable to be of the privy council, or a member of either house of parliament, or to enjoy any office or place of trust, either civil or military, or to have any grant of lands, tenements or hereditaments from the crown, to himself or to any other or others in trust for him.

That no person who has an office or place of profit under the King, or receives a pension from the crown, shall be capable of serving as a member of the house of commons.

That after the said limitation shall take effect as aforesaid, judges' commissions be made *quamdiu se bene gesserint*, and their salaries ascertained and established; but upon the address of both houses of parliament it may be lawful to remove them.

That no pardon under the great seal of England be pleadable to an impeachment by the Commons in Parliament.

Williams (**18**), pp. 58–9.

document 36
Advice on how to manage Parliament, 1690

With the king now financially dependent on Parliament and with Parliament meeting for several months each year, Parliamentary management became more important than ever. However, this letter from Lord Sydney and Thomas Coningsby to William's Dutch favourite, Portland, shows that the techniques used were mostly traditional.

It is without question impossible for a King of England to do any considerable thing in a House of Commons, without a formed management; and by that we mean a number of men on whom the King may confidently rely, joined with the Speaker (who now is most certainly yours) and they to meet privately every night, and there to resolve how and by what methods they will oppose anything which may obstruct His Majesty's affairs, or propose anything that will further his interest the next day; amongst these there ought to be had at any rate two or three men who have fair reputations in the House, such as [William] Sacheverell, Leveson Gower and Sir Thomas Clarges, who must by no means have any employments during the sessions but be rewarded afterwards, and we look upon these three to be those that have the greatest influence over the three parties in the House that are not for king James: Sacheverell of the Whigs, Leveson Gower of the middle party and Sir Thomas Clarges of the High Church; the first of these is so full of himself that we believe it may be a matter difficult enough to secure him, but the other two may most certainly be had...nobody living is better able to give you characters of men fit to serve the King in the House of Commons, and the ways of gaining them, than the Speaker...

Baxter (**20**), pp. 277–8.

document 37
Queen Anne on the threat of party rule

This letter was written to Godolphin in August 1706, as the Whig leaders used their majority in the Commons to put pressure on the queen to admit them to office.

All I desire is my liberty in encouraging and employing all those that concur faithfully in my service, whether they are called Whigs or Tories, not to be tied to one, or to the other, for if I should be so unfortunate as to fall into the hands of either, I shall look upon myself, though I have the name of Queen, to be in reality but their slave, which as it will be my personal ruin, so it will be the destroying of all government, for instead of putting an end to faction, it will lay a lasting foundation for it... .

Why for God's sake must I who have no interest, no end, no thought but for the good of my country, be made so miserable as to be brought into the power of one set of men, and why may I not be trusted, since I mean nothing but what is equally for the good of all my subjects?

Gregg (**58**), p. 223.

document 38
Pressure on Queen Anne to dismiss Harley

By 1708 the Whig leaders had forced their way into office. Now they put pressure on the Queen, through Godolphin and the Duke and Duchess of Marlborough (the Duchess being a rabid Whig), to dismiss her Tory Secretary of State, Robert Harley.

Lord Treasurer [Godolphin] told the Queen he came to resign the staff, that serving her longer with one so perfidious as Mr Harley was impossible; she replied in respect of his long service, she would give him till tomorrow to consider, when he should do as he pleased withal [;] she could find enough glad of that staff.

Then came Lady Duchess with great duty and submission, that she had served her ever with affection and tenderness, &c, her utmost had been her duty and she had been faithful in it. The reply is said to be, 'You shall consider of this till tomorrow, then if you desire it, you shall have leave to retire as you desire... .'

Then entered the Duke, prepared with his utmost address. He told her he had ever served her with obedience and fidelity...that he must lament he came in competition with so vile a creature as Harley; that his fidelity and duty should continue as long as his breath. That it was his duty to be speedy in resigning his commands, that she might put the sword into some other hand immediately, and it was also his duty to tell her he feared the Dutch would immediately on the news make a peace very injurious for England.

'And then, my lord,' says she, 'will you resign me your sword[?]' 'Let me tell you,' says he. 'Your service I have regarded to the utmost of my power.' 'And if you do, my lord, resign your sword, let me tell you, you will run it through my head.'

She went to Council, begging him to follow, he refusing...

Gregg (**58**), pp. 258—9.

Ministerial pressure on George II, 1744
document 39

This account of a discussion between George II and Lord Chancellor Hardwicke illustrates how ministers sought to persuade the king to endorse their policies by arguing that these were in the king's best interests.

King: I have done all you asked of me. I have put all power into your hands and I suppose you will make the most of it.

Chancellor: The disposition of places is not enough if your Majesty takes pains to show the world that you disapprove of your own work.

King: My work! I was forced: I was threatened.

Chancellor: I am sorry to hear your Majesty use those expressions. I know of no force: I know of no threats. No means were used but what has been used in all times, the humble advice of your servants, supported by such reasons as convinced them that the measure was necessary for your service.

King: Yes, I was told I should be opposed.

Chancellor: Never by me, Sir, nor by any of my friends. How others might misrepresent us, I don't pretend to know; but whatever had been our fate, and though Your Majesty had decided on the contrary side to what you did, we would never have gone into an opposition against the necessary measures for carrying on the war and for the support of your government and family.... Taking your money only is not serving you, and nothing can enable one to do that but being put into a possibility and capacity of doing so by your gracious countenance and support.... Your ministers, Sir, are only your instruments of government.

King (smiles): Ministers are the kings in this country.

Costin and Watson (**5**), vol. I, pp. 375—6.

Walpole's advice on managing George II, 1743
document 40

A year after losing office, Walpole advised Henry Pelham on the methods he had used to persuade and influence the king.

This leads me to the most tender and delicate part of the whole; I mean, your behaviour and your manner of treating this subject with him. It is a great misfortune that you have not time; for time and address have often carried things that met, at first onset, with great reluctance; and you must expect to meet the king instructed and greatly prepared in favour of the points which Carteret has in view to drive. Address and management are the weapons you must fight and defend with: plain truths will not be relished at first, in opposition to prejudices conceived and infused in favour of his own partialities; and you must dress up all you offer with the appearance of no other view or tendency but to promote his service in his own way to the utmost of your power. And the more you can make anything appear to be his own, and agreeable to his declarations and orders, given to you before he went, the better you will be heard...

Williams (**18**), pp. 80—81.

document 41
The Pelhams' conditions for returning to office, 1746

After some years in which George II had paid more heed to Lords Bath and Granville than to his ministers, the ministers (led by Henry Pelham and his brother, the Duke of Newcastle) resigned their places. As it soon became clear that Bath and Granville could not establish a majority in the Commons, George had to take the Pelhams back. They laid down the following stipulations before they would resume their offices.

That out of duty to the king and regard to the public, it is apprehended that His Majesty's late servants cannot return into his service without being honoured with that degree of authority, confidence and credit from His Majesty, which the ministers of the crown have usually enjoyed in this country and which is absolutely necessary for carrying on his service. That His Majesty will be pleased entirely to withdraw his confidence and countenance from those persons who of late have, behind the curtain, suggested private counsels, with the view of creating difficulties to his servants, who are responsible for everything, whilst those persons are responsible for nothing.

That His Majesty will be pleased to demonstrate his conviction of mind that those persons have deceived or misled him, by representing that they had sufficient credit and interest in the nation to support and carry on the public affairs, and that he finds they are not able to do it.

That in order to those ends His Majesty will be pleased to remove [certain named persons].

That he will be graciously pleased to perfect the scheme lately humbly proposed to him for bringing Mr Pitt into some honourable employment, and also the other persons formerly named with him.

That His Majesty will be pleased to dispose of the vacant Garters in such manner as to strengthen, and give a public mark of his satisfaction in, his administration.

That, as to foreign affairs, His Majesty will be pleased not to require more from his servants than to support and perfect the plan which he has already approved.

Owen (**94**), pp. 298–9.

document 42
'Country' suspicions of waste and mismanagement, 1689

This account of a Commons debate shows how Tories like Clarges could join with Whigs like Garroway on a 'Country' issue and how 'Country' MPs ignored the figures of official spokesmen, preferring wild allegations of their own.

Sir Thomas Clarges: I think forty thousand men may be taken out of this establishment; I am sure a less number conquered Ireland in 1650. I profess I am much in the dark till I hear some proposition of the king of the state of the war for the next year and till we know the obligation of alliances. The Dutch forces are given in fourteen thousand. They are not all in Ireland, some are in Scotland. They are upon parole to keep up 70 in a company &c and perhaps they are but 32 in a company... .

The Earl of Ranelagh [Paymaster of the Army] gives an account of the establishment and rectifies Clarges' mistakes.

William Garroway: I see no certainty of the number of men in England, Scotland and Ireland. I think the account that has been transferred to you comes from the muster-master and the king is abused. I would go on regularly to the state of the war, what the king thinks fitting and they to bring in where the men are; without the certain number of men, you know not how to provide. I think it fitter to apply to the fleet and retrench the land men. England knows no need of them. I believe the money is not all spent. I think it may be embezzled. I never saw a worse account... . I would have accounts brought here by somebody that will allow them, but I desire not to go blindfold. Let the money be rightly applied and I will go with the highest and I desire the king to give us the state of the war.

Grey (7), vol. IX, pp. 389−90.

document 43
'Country' suspicion of placemen, 1691

Thompson was at this time one of the most forthright 'Country' speakers among the Whigs. Although he held office for a while under William, his 'Country' principles led him to become a Tory, if a somewhat eccentric one, under Anne.

Sir John Thompson: I could wish we had a self-denying ordinance 'that no persons should sit here that have places or offices of profit'. I am justified by good authority; for before Henry VIII's time, no person that belonged to the court was permitted to sit within these walls. 'Tis wonderful to consider that, when the Commons were poorer than now, they should remove great men and favourites from the crown. The reason then was, there was no dependency upon the court; they brought more of the country and less of the court with them [than] in after times. I speak my mind truly and have no reserves, but I believe we shall not carry this, because there were never more dependencies on the court than now.

Grey (7), vol. X, p. 215.

document 44
'Country' hostility to standing armies, 1697

After the Peace of Ryswick in 1697, William did not wish to disband the forces raised for the war, because he believed that war was likely to break out at any moment over the Spanish succession. This excited 'Country' suspicion (found among Whigs as well as Tories) that he wished to use the army to make himself absolute. The standing army controversy caused the most serious political crisis of the reign and provoked a flood of pamphlets. The following is taken from one of the best known, written by two Whigs.

Our constitution depending upon a due balance between King, Lords and Commons, and that balance depending upon the mutual occasions and necessities they have of one another; if this cement be once broke, there is an actual dissolution of the government. Now this balance can never be preserved but by an union of the natural and artificial strength of the kingdom, that is, by making the militia to consist of the same persons as have the property; or otherwise the government is violent and against nature and cannot possibly continue, but the constitution must either break the army or the army will destroy the constitution: for it is universally true that wherever the militia is, there is or will be the government in a short time... .

The detestable policies of the last reigns were with the utmost art and application to disarm the people and make the militia useless, to countenance a standing army in order to bring in Popery and slavery... . Why may not the nobility, gentry and freeholders of England be trusted with the defence of their own lives, estates and liberties, without having guardians and keepers assigned them? And why may they not defend them with as much vigour and courage as mercenaries who have nothing to lose?...

J. Trenchard and W. Moyle, *An Argument Showing that a Standing Army is Inconsistent with a Free Government,* 1697, reprinted by The Rota, Exeter, 1971, pp. 4, 20–21.

document 45
The Tories' motives on coming to power in 1710

This extract from a pamphlet by Bolingbroke shows clearly how the pursuit of power and profit and the pursuit of political principle intertwined and reinforced one another. It is also a striking statement of the belief that the Tories were the natural majority party.

I am afraid that we came to court in the same dispositions as all parties have done; that the principal spring of our actions was to have the government of the state in our hands; that our principal views were the conservation of this power, great employments to ourselves, and great opportunities of rewarding those who had helped to raise us, and of hurting those who stood in opposition to us. It is however true, that with these considerations of private and party interest there were others intermingled, which had for their object the public good of the nation, at least what we took to be such.

We looked on the political principles which had generally prevailed in our government from the Revolution in 1688, to be destructive of our true interest, to have mingled us too much in the affairs of the continent, to tend to the impoverishing our people and to the loosening the bands of our constitution in Church and State. We supposed the Tory party to be the bulk of the landed interest, and to have no contrary influence blended into its composition. We supposed the Whigs to be the remains of a party, formed against the ill designs of the Court under King Charles II, nursed up into strength and applied to contrary uses by King William III, and yet still so weak as to lean for support on the Presbyterians and other sectaries, on the Bank and the other corporations, on the Dutch and the other allies. From hence we judged it to follow that they had been forced, and must continue so, to render the national interest subservient to the interest of those who lent them an additional strength, without which they could never be the prevalent party. The view, therefore, of those amongst us who thought in this manner, was to improve the Queen's favour to break the body of the Whigs, to render their supports useless to them and to fill the employments of the kingdom, down to the meanest, with Tories.

Holmes and Speck (**10**), pp. 141–2.

document 46
Exploitation of 'Country' sensibilities for party ends, 1692

This extract from a debate on naval miscarriages shows how Whig politicians tried to blame those miscarriages on the Tory Earl of Nottingham's allegedly lukewarm commitment to William's regime: in other words, they sought to stigmatize Nottingham's administrative shortcomings as political disloyalty and to use 'Country' resentment at naval failure to attack a political opponent. It also shows that, in mixed ministries, there was a danger of office-holders dividing along party lines.

John Smith: ...There is a coolness in people's minds to this government which arises, I think, because they believe you have not a rightful king but only *de facto* and that if King James comes back they may return to their allegiance to him. Hence arises your mischief and this, I think, ought to be your first head of advice.

Thomas Wharton, Comptroller of the Household: The gentleman that spoke last has touched upon the true cause of your grievance; it lies deeper than you are aware of. Your chief men that manage matters are such as submit to this king upon wrong principles — because he has the governing power — but will be as ready to join another if he prevails. They are such as came not into your government till it was late, and I think it no policy to take men into a government because they were violent against it. I would not at present name these persons but I would address His Majesty against them in general (for he knows them best) and that he would be pleased to receive such men only under him who are of known integrity and will come up both to the principles and His Majesty's right to this government... .

A motion was made by the friends to the Lord Nottingham that all the papers and letters relating to the descent might be laid before this House. But it was opposed by his enemies, the Whigs; so carried in the negative.

Luttrell (**13**), pp. 274, 277.

document 47
A Tory's reasons for swearing allegiance to William

Tories like Sir John Bramston had very mixed feelings in 1689. They did not want their rightful king (James) to return, but felt most reluctant to recognize William as king de jure. Most, like Bramston, were prepared to swear allegiance to William as king de facto: after all, they argued, government had to be carried on by someone. They thus salved their consciences by using arguments whose pragmatism had much in common with those of the Whigs (see **document 23**).

I did think, as the circumstances of the government then were, by the King James leaving the kingdom as he did without any commission or care taken for preservation of his subjects, private men, if required upon penalties, might safely swear to the oath of allegiance prescribed... . By the king absenting himself and leaving the kingdom without any governor or commissioner, it was impossible for us to pay allegiance to him according to our oath, which oath therefore is become as to us abrogated, or at least during his absence is in abeyance... . We that are private persons cannot judge whether his absence be voluntary or forced... . By his absence it became necessary that government should be by somebody, to avoid confusion. There can be no government without submission to it, that can, whether by one or more, have no assurance of submission but by a religious tie and obligation; the constant practice in all states is by oath to oblige obedience. When the government is fixed, obedience becomes necessary to it, and conscience obliges private persons to yield obedience, as well as prudence and safety to prevent anarchy, and the rabble from spoiling and robbing the noble and wealthy. These assertions and reasons seem to me to arise out of pure necessity.

Autobiography of Sir John Bramston, ed. Lord Braybrooke, Camden Society, 1845, p. 355.

document 48

Modification of Tory views on non-resistance

The Tory argument that submission was due to a king de facto *implied, logically, that submission was due to* any *established regime, as can be seen in this extract from a sermon of 1700.*

That there is such a submission due from all subjects to the Supreme Authority of the place wherein they live, as shall tie up their hands from opposing or resisting it by force, is evident from the very nature and ends of political society. And I dare say there is not that country on earth, let the form of government be what it will (Absolute Monarchy, Legal Monarchy, Aristocracy or Commonwealth) where this is not a part of the constitution. Subjects must obey passively where they cannot obey actively, otherwise the government would be precarious, and the public peace at the mercy of every malcontent, and a door would be set open to all the insurrections, rebellions and treasons in the world.

Kenyon (**79**), p. 54.

document 49

Rival views on foreign policy, 1692

Clarges and Wharton here state succinctly the Tory and Whig positions on foreign policy.

Sir Thomas Clarges: Why we should be at a greater charge than our treaties oblige us to, I see no reason for. I know it is a received opinion with the Dutch and the Germans that England is an inexhaustible fountain, but if you go on at the rate you have I am afraid you will quickly be drawn dry. The security of this nation, with our interest, lies in having a good fleet at sea and, if we can, to destroy that of our enemies, and not to send armies abroad, which will drain the nation both of our people and our money too... .

Goodwin Wharton: Consider with yourself; if he [Louis XIV] swallows Flanders, Holland must follow and if France be once master of Holland, pray think what will become of you. Will your fleet be able to deal with that of France and Holland too, for that will be the consequence.

Luttrell (**13**), pp. 288, 291.

Bibliography

PRIMARY SOURCES

1 Browning, A. (ed.), *English Historical Documents, 1660–1714*, Eyre & Spottiswoode, 1953

2 Burnet, G., *History of My Own Time*, 6 vols, Oxford U.P., 1833

3 Burnet, G., *Supplement to Burnet's History of My Own Time*, ed. H.C. Foxcroft, Oxford U.P., 1902

4 Clarendon, Earl of (H. Hyde), *Correspondence and Diaries*, ed. S.W. Singer, 2 vols, London, 1828

5 Costin, W.C., and Watson, J.S. (eds), *The Law and Working of the Constitution*, vol. I, 1660–1783, Black, 1952

6 Dalrymple, Sir J., *Memoirs of Great Britain and Ireland*, 2 vols, London, 1771–3

7 Grey, A., *Debates in the House of Commons, 1667–94*, 10 vols, London, 1769

8 Halifax, Marquis of (G. Savile), *Complete Works*, ed. J.P. Kenyon, Penguin, 1969

9 Halifax, Marquis of (G. Savile), *Life and Letters*, ed. H.C. Foxcroft, 2 vols, Longman, 1898

10 Holmes, G., and Speck, W.A. (eds), *The Divided Society: Parties and Politics in England, 1694–1716*, Arnold, 1967

11 Kenyon, J.P., *The Stuart Constitution*, Cambridge U.P., 1966

12 Locke, J., *Two Treatises of Government*, ed. P. Laslett, Mentor, 1965

13 Luttrell, N., *Parliamentary Diary, 1691–3*, ed. H. Horwitz, Oxford U.P., 1972

14 *Parliamentary History*, ed. W. Cobbett, vol. V, 1688–1702, London, 1809

15 Reresby, Sir J., *Memoirs*, ed. A. Browning, Jackson, 1936

16 Schwoerer, L.G., 'A Jornall of the Convention at Westminster Begun the 22 of January, 1688/9', *Bulletin of the Institute of Historical Research*, vol. XLIX, 1976

17 Simpson, A., 'Notes of a Noble Lord, 22 January to 12 February, 1689', *English Historical Review*, vol. LII, 1937

18 Williams, E.N., *The Eighteenth Century Constitution*, Cambridge U.P., 1960

SECONDARY WORKS

19 Baxter, S., *The Development of the Treasury, 1660–1702*, Longman, 1957

20 Baxter, S., *William III*, Longman, 1966

21 Beckett, J.C., *The Making of Modern Ireland*, Faber, 1966

22 Beddard, R., 'The Guildhall Declaration of 11 December 1688 and the Counter-Revolution of the Loyalists', *Historical Journal*, vol. XI, 1968

23 Behrens, B., 'The Whig Theory of the Constitution in the Reign of Charles II', *Cambridge Historical Journal*, vol. VII, 1941

24 Bennett, G.V., *The Tory Crisis in Church and State, 1688–1730*, Oxford U.P., 1975

25 Bennett, G.V., and Walsh, J.D. (eds), *Essays in Modern English Church History in Memory of Norman Sykes*, Black, 1966

26 Bolam, C.G., Goring, J.J., Short, H.L., and Thomas, R., *The English Presbyterians*, Allen & Unwin, 1968

27 Brooks, C., 'Public Finance and Political Stability: The Administration of the Land Tax, 1688–1720', *Historical Journal*, vol. XVII, 1974

28 Browning, A., *Thomas, Earl of Danby*, 3 vols, Jackson, 1951

29 Burton, I.F., Riley, P.W.J., and Rowlands, E., 'Political Parties in the Reigns of William III and Anne: The Evidence of Division Lists', *Bulletin of the Institute of Historical Research*, Special Supplement 7, 1968

30 Cannon, J. (ed.), *The Whig Ascendancy*, Arnold, 1981

31 Carswell, J., *The Descent on England*, Barrie-Cressett, 1969

32 Chandaman, C.D., *The English Public Revenue, 1660–88*, Oxford U.P., 1975

33 Cherry, G.L., 'The Legal and Philosophical Position of the Jacobites, 1688–9', *Journal of Modern History*, vol. XXII, 1950

34 Childs, J., *The Army, James II and the Glorious Revolution*, Manchester, 1980

35 Christie, I.R., *Myth and Reality in Late Eighteenth Century British Politics*, Macmillan, 1970

36 Clapham, Sir J., *The Bank of England*, vol. I, Cambridge U.P., 1970

37 Clarkson, L.A., *The Pre-Industrial Economy, 1500–1750*, Batsford, 1971

38 Coward, B., *The Stuart Age*, Longman, 1980

39 Cragg, G.R., *From Puritanism to the Age of Reason*, Cambridge, 1950

40 Davies, G., *Essays on the Later Stuarts*, Huntington Library, 1958

41 Davis, R., *A Commercial Revolution*, Historical Association, 1967

42 Dickinson, H.T., *Liberty and Property: Political Ideology in Eighteenth Century Britain*, Methuen, 1979

43 Dickson, P.G.M., *The Financial Revolution in England, 1688–1756*, Macmillan, 1967

44 Donaldson, G., *Scotland, James V to James VII*, Oliver & Boyd, 1965

45 Downie, J.A., 'The•Commission of Public Accounts and the Formation of the Country Party', *English Historical Review*, vol. XCI, 1976

46 Dunn, J., *The Political Thought of John Locke*, Cambridge U.P., 1969

47 Earle, P., *Monmouth's Rebels*, Weidenfeld & Nicolson, 1977

48 Earle, P., *The World of Defoe*, Weidenfeld & Nicolson, 1976

49 Feiling, K.G., *History of the Tory Party, 1640–1714*, Oxford U.P., 1924

50 Ferguson, W., *Scotland, 1689 to the Present*, Oliver & Boyd, 1968

51 Figgis, J.N., *The Divine Right of Kings*, Harper & Row, 1965

52 Frankle, R.J., 'The Formulation of the Declaration of Rights', *Historical Journal*, vol. XVII, 1974

53 Garrett, J., *The Triumphs of Providence: The Assassination Plot of 1696*, Cambridge U.P., 1980

54 Gilbert, A.D., *Religion and Society in Industrial England*, Longman, 1976

55 Glassey, L., *Politics and the Appointment of Justices of the Peace, 1675–1720*, Oxford U.P., 1979

56 Gough, J.W., *Fundamental Law in English Constitutional History*, Oxford U.P., 1955

57 Gough, J.W., *The Social Contract*, 2nd edn, Oxford U.P., 1957

58 Gregg, E., *Queen Anne*, Routledge & Kegan Paul, 1980

59 Haley, K.H.D., *The Dutch in the Seventeenth Century*, Thames & Hudson, 1972

60 Havighurst, A.F., 'James II and the Twelve Men in Scarlet', *Law Quarterly Review*, vol. LXIX, 1953

61 Havighurst, A.F., 'The Judiciary and Politics in the Reign of Charles II', *Law Quarterly Review*, vol. LXVI, 1950

62 Hazard, P., *The European Mind, 1680–1715*, Penguin, 1964

63 Hill, B.W., *The Growth of Parliamentary Parties, 1689—1742*, Allen & Unwin, 1976

64 Holmes, G. (ed.), *Britain after the Glorious Revolution, 1689—1714*, Macmillan, 1969

65 Holmes, G., *British Politics in the Age of Anne*, Macmillan, 1967

66 Holmes, G., *The Electorate and the National Will in the First Age of Party*, Inaugural Lecture, Lancaster, 1975

67 Holmes, G., *The Trial of Dr Sacheverell*, Methuen, 1973

68 Horwitz, H., 'Parliament and the Glorious Revolution', *Bulletin of the Institute of Historical Research*, vol. XLVII, 1974

69 Horwitz, H., *Parliament, Policy and Politics in the Reign of William III*, Manchester, 1977

70 Horwitz, H., *Revolution Politicks: The Career of Daniel Finch, Second Earl of Nottingham*, Cambridge U.P., 1968

71 Jones, G.H., *The Main Stream of Jacobitism*, Harvard U.P., 1954

72 Jones, J.R., *Country and Court: England 1658—1714*, Arnold, 1978

73 Jones, J.R., *The First Whigs*, Oxford, 1961

74 Jones, J.R. (ed.), *The Restored Monarchy*, Macmillan, 1979

75 Jones, J.R., *The Revolution of 1688 in England*, Weidenfeld & Nicolson, 1972

76 Kemp, B., *King and Commons, 1660—1832*, Macmillan, 1957

77 Kenyon, J.P., 'The Earl of Sunderland and the King's Administration', *English Historical Review*, vol. LXXI, 1956

78 Kenyon, J.P., *The Nobility in the Revolution of 1688*, Inaugural Lecture, Hull, 1963

79 Kenyon, J.P., 'The Revolution of 1688: Resistance and Contract', in N. McKendrick (ed.), *Historical Perspectives: Studies in English Thought and Society in Honour of J.H. Plumb*, Europa, 1974

80 Kenyon, J.P., *Revolution Principles: The Politics of Party, 1689—1720*, Cambridge U.P., 1977

81 Kenyon, J.P., *Robert Spencer, Earl of Sunderland*, Longman, 1958

82 Kramnick, I., *Bolingbroke and his Circle: The Politics of Nostalgia in the Age of Walpole*, Harvard, 1968

83 Langford, P., *The Excise Crisis*, Oxford, 1975

84 Lenman, B., *The Jacobite Risings in Britain, 1689—1746*, Eyre Methuen, 1980

85 Macaulay, T.B., *History of England*, ed. C.H. Firth, 6 vols, Macmillan, 1913

86 MacInnes, A., *Robert Harley*, Gollancz, 1970

87 Miller, J., 'Charles II and his Parliaments', *Transactions of the Royal Historical Society*, 5th Series, vol. XXXII, 1982

88 Miller, J., 'The Glorious Revolution: "Contract" and "Abdication" Reconsidered', *Historical Journal*, vol. 25, 1982

89 Miller, J., *James II: A Study in Kingship*, Wayland, 1978

90 Miller, J., *Popery and Politics in England, 1660−88*, Cambridge U.P., 1973

91 Namier, L.B., *The Structure of Politics at the Accession of George III*, 2nd edn, Macmillan, 1957

92 Ogg, D., *England in the Reign of Charles II*, 2nd edn, Oxford U.P., 1956

93 Ogg, D., *England in the Reigns of James II and William III*, Oxford U.P., 1955

94 Owen, J.B., *The Rise of the Pelhams*, Methuen, 1957

95 Pinkham, L.B., *William III and the Respectable Revolution*, Harvard U.P., 1954

96 Plumb, J.H., 'Elections to the Convention Parliament of 1689', *Cambridge Historical Journal*, vol. V, 1937

97 Plumb, J.H., *The Growth of Political Stability in England, 1675−1725*, Macmillan, 1967

98 Plumb, J.H., *Sir Robert Walpole*, 2 vols, Cresset, 1950−56

99 Pocock, J.G.A., *The Ancient Constitution and the Feudal Law*, Cambridge U.P., 1957

100 Reitan, E.A., 'From Revenue to Civil List, 1689−1702', *Historical Journal*, vol. XIII, 1970

101 Riley, P.W.J., *The Union of England and Scotland*, Manchester U.P., 1979

102 Roberts, C., 'The Constitutional Significance of the Financial Settlement of 1690,' *Historical Journal*, vol. XX, 1977

103 Roberts, C., *The Growth of Responsible Government in Stuart England*, Cambridge U.P., 1966

104 Roseveare, H., *The Treasury: The Evolution of a British Institution*, Allen Lane, 1969

105 Roseveare, H., *The Treasury: The Foundations of Control*, Allen & Unwin, 1973

106 Simms, J.G., *Jacobite Ireland, 1685−91*, Routledge & Kegan Paul, 1969

107 Skinner, Q.R.D., 'History and Ideology in the English Revolution', *Historical Journal*, vol. VIII, 1965

108 Speck, W.A., *Stability and Strife: England, 1714−60*, Arnold, 1977

109 Speck, W.A., *Tory and Whig: The Struggle in the Constituencies, 1701–15*, Macmillan, 1970

110 Sykes, N., *Church and State in England in the Eighteenth Century*, Cambridge U.P., 1934

111 Sykes, N., *From Sheldon to Secker*, Cambridge U.P., 1959

112 Taylor, G., *The Problem of Poverty, 1660–1834*, Longman, 1969

113 Thomas, R., 'Comprehension and Indulgence', in G.F. Nuttall and O. Chadwick (eds), *From Uniformity to Unity, 1662–1962*, SPCK 1962

114 Tomlinson, H., *Guns and Government: The Ordnance Office Under the Later Stuarts*, Royal Historical Society, 1979

115 Trevelyan, G.M., *The English Revolution, 1688–9*, Oxford U.P., 1938

116 Western, J.R., *Monarchy and Revolution: The English State in the Sixteen Eighties*, Blandford, 1972

117 Wickham Legg, J., *English Church Life from the Restoration to the Tractarian Movement*, Longman, 1914

118 Wilson, C., *England's Apprenticeship, 1603–1763*, Longman, 1965

Index

reason as logic
or motivation
or a way of life

NB half-baked tolerance
because one doesn't care.